SCOTLAND'S GARDENS SCHEME 1997

Contents

FRONT COVER PHOTOGRAPH

Fallen leaves of *Acer trautvetteri* lie in a stream bed at Dawyck Botanic Garden, Peeblesshire. *A. trautvetteri*, the Red-bud Maple, uncommon in Britain outwith specialist collections, is a native of the Caucasus, Asiatic Turkey and Iran. In spring it is adorned with brilliant crimson bud-scales, and in autumn has showy large-winged rosy-coloured fruits.

Photograph by Sidney J. Clarke, FRPS,
Principal Photographer at the Royal Botanic Garden Edinburgh.
Illustrations by Steven Carroll.

Printed by Inglis Allen, 40 Townsend Place, Kirkcaldy, Fife

CHAIRMAN'S MESSAGE

As the new Chairman of Scotland's Gardens Scheme, about to embark on what I am certain will be five exciting and stimulating years, I am glad to begin my message by paying tribute to Barbara Findlay, our retiring Chairman.

During her period as Chairman she visited practically every garden which opens under the Scheme, inspiring one and all with her interest and enthusiasm. Her aim was to get the name of Scotland's Gardens Scheme better known, and this she has more than succeeded in doing, if our record total of £304,815 is anything to go by.

We have been delighted by the success of the Art Exhibition which she set up, generously sponsored by Adam & Company, and staged in conjunction with the Royal Botanic Garden Edinburgh, when artists were invited to submit paintings of any garden which opened for the Scheme in 1996.

Finally, I should like to urge you to take cameras when garden visiting this year and enter the competition sponsored by Phillips Scotland, Auctioneers, further details of which can be found opposite page 65.

Kirsty Maxwell Stuart

❖❖

SCOTLAND'S GARDENS SCHEME HISTORY

Scotland's Gardens Scheme was founded on 23rd March 1931 at a garden owners' meeting called to help raise £2,000 which the Queen's Nursing Institute needed to fund the rapid expansion of district nursing. The Queen Mother, then the Duchess of York, lent her support, while King George V promised that the Balmoral gardens would open for the Scheme, with a generous annual contribution still being made today.

Under the inaugural chairmanship of the Countess of Minto, a central committee with a network of volunteer organisers throughout Scotland was formed, much the shape of the Scheme today. £1,000 was raised in the first year, double that in the next, and by 1939 over £22,000 was contributed. Even during the war proceeds increased, helped by the addition of flower and produce stalls and the provision of teas.

Although the training duties of the Queen's Nursing Institute were taken over by the National Health Service, many elderly nurses still receive our support. In 1952 the Gardens Fund of the National Trust for Scotland became our other main beneficiary, so that we could help to preserve the great gardens of historical importance in Scotland. In 1961 it was agreed that garden owners might select a registered charity to which up to 40% of the gross takings from their garden opening could be donated. This benefits over 140 different charities each year and is unique to Scotland's Gardens Scheme.

Over the years the Scheme has enabled millions of people to enjoy the beautiful gardens of Scotland and we hope, with your help, many more will do so for years to come.

A MESSAGE FROM
THE QUEEN'S NURSING INSTITUTE, SCOTLAND

Our thanks go to all those who have toiled to make this past year a record one enabling us to receive the largest donation ever, £46,445, to assist with schemes bringing **Nursing Care into the Home.**

The outreach work done by **Rachel House**, the new **Children's Hospice** at Kinross, will continue, whilst excellent results have been achieved by the **Diabetic Nurse** working in the Lothians and the **Cardiac Rehabilitation Nurse** in Stirling. New projects underway range from assessing new methods for **Treatment of Leg Ulcers** in Shetland, providing **Clinical Support for Nurses in Remote Locations** in Argyll to a **Public Health Nurse** working with teenagers in a Vale of Leven Health Promotion project.

The annual Innovation Awards started in 1991 to encourage Community Nurses to put new ideas into practice are now well recognised. This year we are supporting non-medication **Adult Sleep Clinics** in Dundee, **collaborative working in Community Assessment** by nurses and social workers in West Lothian, a **Teenage Health Clinic** in Oban and helping care assistants in Shetland **to support the terminally ill.**

A leaflet outlining the work of the Queen's Nursing Institute Scotland is available from the Institute. We are fully aware that our ability not only to assist hard pressed nurses with these projects, but also to support retired Queen's Nurses as well as making a positive contribution to the further education of Community Nurses, is dependent on the generosity of all those who contribute to Scotland's Gardens Scheme in so many different ways.

A sunny year indeed — here's to another one!

George Preston   The Queen's Nursing Institute
Secretary & Treasurer   31 Castle Terrace, Edinburgh EH1 2EL

A MESSAGE TO GARDEN OWNERS FROM

♛ The National Trust for Scotland

I am most grateful to Scotland's Gardens Scheme for once again giving me the opportunity to express the sincere thanks of The National Trust for Scotland to all those associated with running Scotland's Gardens Scheme and to the owners of private gardens for all their hard work and dedication throughout the year. These wonderful efforts, which benefit so many charities including The National Trust for Scotland, provide extremely generous and much welcomed financial assistance. Maintaining gardens in a tip top condition is a costly business which is why the owners' contribution to the Trust's Gardens Fund is so important and so greatly appreciated.

1996 has been another eventful year, but in this short message I can only mention two highlights for the Trust. In May the American Rhododendron Society held its annual convention in Oban and the Trust was delighted to welcome a great many delegates to our gardens at Arduaine, Brodick and Gigha. It was a perfect week weather-wise and the delegates were much impressed, not only by Trust gardens but by all the other gardens in the area. In October, as a gesture of thanks, the Trust was delighted to welcome 120 Scotland's Gardens Scheme owners to a "Day of Lectures" at Dalmeny. The speakers were Roy Lancaster, Jim McColl and David Stuart, who were all entertaining as well as informative, which made for a most enjoyable day.

The Trust owes a very great deal to Scotland's Gardens Scheme and especially to those garden owners who select us as the charity of their choice. I would like to stress how sincerely grateful we are for all your suppport. We send renewed thanks to all those who take part in the Scheme and our best wishes for good gardening results in 1997.

Douglas Dow
Director

The Gardeners' Royal Benevolent Society in Scotland

An Exempt Charity Registered under the Industrial & Provident Societies Act 1974. Number 15408R.

The GRBS currently assists some 500 beneficiaries with regular quarterly payments and invites applications from other retired gardeners and their spouses interested in becoming a beneficiary of the Society. Help is also given from the Good Samaritan Fund for unexpected expenses and special needs. Sheltered housing is offered in three locations in England and Red Oaks, the Society's home at Henfield in Sussex, offers residential and nursing care. In Scotland, Netherbyres near Eyemouth, which opened its doors to retired gardeners in 1993 is now well established.

In 1995 the number of Regional Organisers in Scotland rose to five, thus bringing the Gardeners' Royal Benevolent Society to many more people throughout the country. Please look out for the Society's Regional Organisers at gardening events during the year, they would be very glad to meet you.

For further information please contact Miss May Wardlaw, GRBS Regional Organiser, c/o SGS, 31 Castle Terrace, Edinburgh EH1 2EL *or* The Gardeners' Royal Benevolent Society, Bridge House, 139 Kingston Road, Leatherhead, Surrey KT22

THE ROYAL GARDENERS' ORPHAN FUND

Registered Charity No. 248746

We are glad to have this opportunity once again to thank Scotland's Gardens Scheme for its valued annual donation to our Fund.

Over the past year we have helped six orphaned children in Scotland by way of regular quarterly allowances and have assisted a further nine needy children, including a lad of eleven severely handicapped by cerebral palsy and the two young children of a gardener permanently disabled following an accident at work.

Our Secretary visits these children and their families each year, thus keeping our Committee in touch with each child's progress and particular needs. Should you wish to know more of our work please contact our Secretary, Mrs Kate Wallis, at the address detailed below.

48 St Albans Road
Codicote, Hitchen
Herts SG4 8UT
Tel: 01438 820783

GENERAL INFORMATION

Houses are not open unless specifically stated; where the house or part of the house is shown, an additional charge is usually made.

Lavatories. Private gardens do not normally have outside lavatories. Regrettably, for security reasons, owners have been advised not to admit visitors into their houses.

Dogs. Unless otherwise stated, dogs are usually admitted, but only if kept on a lead. They are not admitted to houses.

Teas. When teas are available this is indicated in the text. An extra charge is usually made for refreshments.

Professional Photographers. No photographs taken in a garden may be used for sale or reproduction without the prior permission of the garden owner.

 ♿ Denotes gardens suitable for wheelchairs.

\# Denotes gardens opening for the first time or re-opening after several years.

The National Trust for Scotland. Members are requested to note that where a National Trust property has allocated an opening day to Scotland's Gardens Scheme which is one of its own normal opening days, members can gain entry on production of their Trust membership card, although donations to Scotland's Gardens Scheme will be most welcome.

Children. All children must be accompanied by an adult.

SCOTLAND'S GARDENS SCHEME
Charity No. SC011337

We welcome gardens large and small and also groups of gardens.
If you would like information on how to open your garden for charity
please contact us at the address below.

SCOTLAND'S GARDENS SCHEME,
31 CASTLE TERRACE, EDINBURGH
Telephone: 0131 229 1870   Fax: 0131 229 0443

NAME & ADDRESS: (Block capitals please) ....

....

....

.... Post Code ....

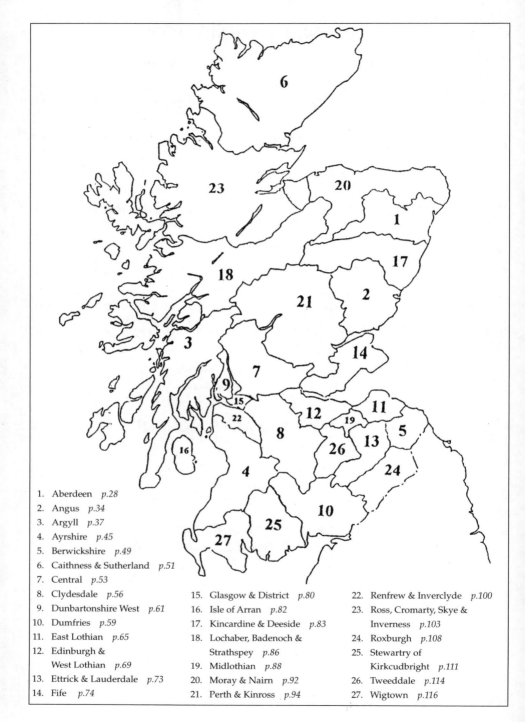

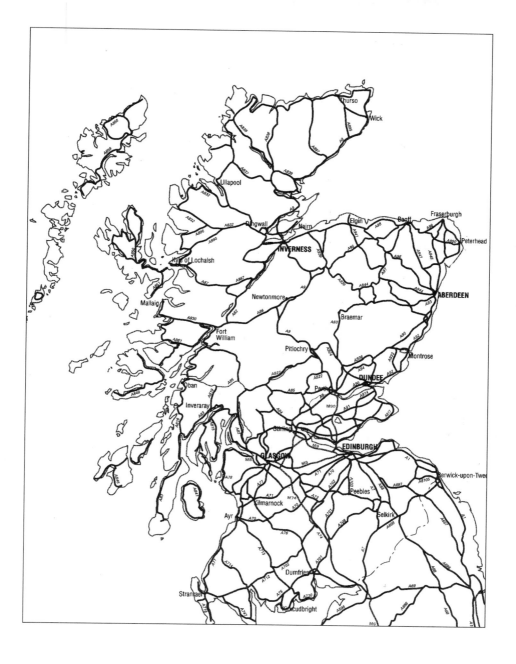

THE GARDENS LISTED BELOW OPEN FOR SCOTLAND'S GARDENS SCHEME ON A REGULAR BASIS, OR BY APPOINTMENT.

FULL DETAILS ARE GIVEN IN THE DISTRICT LIST OF GARDENS

ABERDEEN

23 Don Street, Old Aberdeen   *Daily April-September by appointment: 01224 487269*
#Greenridge, Cults   *July & August by appointment: 01224 860200*
Kirkstile House, Gartly   *May to August by appointment: 01466 720243*
Nether Affloch Farmhouse, Dunecht   *July & August by appointment: 01330 860362*
Old Semeil Herb Garden, Strathdon   *May to August 10am - 5pm*
Station Cottage, Gartly   *June - August by appointment: 01466 720277*

ANGUS

House of Pitmuies, Guthrie,   *Daily Easter – 31 October 10am-5pm*

ARGYLL

Achnacloich, Connel   *Daily 24 March -31 October 10am - 6pm*
An Cala, Ellenabeich   *Daily 1 April-15 October 10am - 6pm*
#Appin House, Appin   *Daily 14 April - 12 October 10am - 6pm*
Ardanaiseig, Lochaweside   *Daily all year 9am - 5pm*
Ardchattan Priory, North Connel   *Daily 1 April-30 October 9am - 6pm*
Ardkinglas Woodland Garden, Cairndow   *Daily all year*
Ardmaddy Castle, Balvicar   *Daily 1 April-31 October or by appt: 01852 300353*
Barguillean's 'Angus Garden', Taynuilt   *Daily all year*
Coille Dharaich, Kilmelford   *By appointment: 01852 200285*
Crarae Glen Garden, Minard   *Daily April-October 9am - 6pm*
Crinan Hotel Garden, Crinan   *Daily 30 April - 30 September*
Dalnaheish, Tayvallich   *April-September by appointment: 01546 870286*
Druimavuic House, Appin   *Daily 13 April-29 June 10am - 6 pm*
Druimneil House, Port Appin   *Daily 28 March-19 June 9am - 6pm*
Eredine Woodland Garden, Lochaweside   *Saturdays all year, except 14 June, 11am - 4pm*
Glenfeochan House Hotel, Kilmore   *Daily 15 March-31 October 10am - 6pm*
Jura House, Isle of Jura   *Open all year 9am - 5pm*
Kildalloig, Campbeltown   *By appointment: 01586 553192*
Kinlochlaich House Gardens, Appin   *Open all year 9.30am-5.30pm or dusk (except Suns Oct-March)*
                                       Sundays April - Sept. 10.30am - 5.30pm
Mount Stuart, Isle of Bute *2 May - 12 October (not Tues & Thurs) 10am-5pm.*
Tighnamara, Kilmelford   *By appointment spring - autumn: 01852 200224*
Torosay Castle & Gardens, Isle of Mull   *Open all year. Summer 9am - 7pm.Winter, sunrise - sunset*

AYRSHIRE

#Bargany, Girvan   *1 March-31 October 10am-7pm or dusk*
Blair, Dalry   *All year round*

BERWICKSHIRE

Bughtrig, Leitholm   *June – September 11am-5pm or by appointment: 01890 840678*
The Hirsel, Coldstream   *Open daily all year reasonable daylight hours*
Manderston, Duns   *Sundays & Thursdays 18 May-28 September*

CENTRAL

Daldrishaig House, Aberfoyle   *May to July by appointment: 01877 382223*
Kilbryde Castle   *All year by appointment: 01786 823104*

CLYDESDALE

Baitlaws, Lamington   *July & August by appointment: 01899 850240*
Biggar Park, Biggar   *May to August by appointment: 01899 220185*

DUMFRIES

Arbigland, Kirkbean   *Tuesdays-Sundays: May-September 2-6pm Also Bank Holiday Mondays*

DUNBARTONSHIRE WEST

Auchendarroch, Tarbet   *1 April – 30 June by appointment: 01301 702240*
Glenarn, Rhu   *Daily 21 March-21 July, Sunrise to Sunset*

EDINBURGH & WEST LOTHIAN

Newliston, Kirkliston   *Wednesdays-Sundays incl. 1 May- 4 June 2-6pm*

FIFE

Cambo House, Kingsbarns   *Daily all year 10am-5pm*

GLASGOW

Invermay, Cambuslang   *April – September by appointment: 0141 641 1632*

KINCARDINE & DEESIDE

Shooting Greens, Strachan   *27 April – 12 May by appointment: 01330 850221*

MIDLOTHIAN

Arniston, Gorebridge   *Tuesdays, Thursdays & Sundays July-mid September*
Greenfield Lodge, Lasswade   *First Tuesday of each month March-September incl. 2-5pm,*
or by appointment: 0131 663 9338
The Mill House, Temple   *Second Wednesday of each month April-September incl. 2-5pm*
Newhall, Carlops   *Tuesdays to Thursdays, April - October. Glen 1-5pm Walled Garden 2-5pm*

PERTH AND KINROSS

Ardvorlich, Lochearnhead   *11 May - 8 June 2 - 6pm*
Bolfracks, Aberfeldy   *Daily 28 March -31 October 10am - 6pm*
Cluny House, Aberfeldy   *Daily 1 March-31 October 10am - 6pm*
Drummond Castle Gardens, Muthill   *Daily May-October 2 - 6pm, last entrance 5pm*
Lude, Blair Atholl   *20 June - 6 August, by appointment: 01796 481240*
Scone Palace, Perth   *28 March - 13 October 9.30am - 5pm*

ROSS, CROMARTY, SKYE & INVERNESS

Abriachan Garden Nursery, Loch Ness side   *February-November 9am - dusk*
Attadale, Strathcarron   *Easter - end October, not Suns 10am-5pm*
Clan Donald, Isle of Skye   *Daily all year*
Coiltie, Divach, Drumnadrochit   *Daily June-August 12-7pm*
Dunvegan Castle, Isle of Skye   *17 March-31 October 10am-5.30pm, last entry 5pm*
Glamaig, Isle of Skye   *Daily Easter to mid September*
House of Aigas & Field Centre, by Beauly   *Daily mid June- September*
Leckmelm Shrubbery & Arboretum by Ullapool   *Daily 1 April-30 September 10am - 6pm*
Sea View, Dundonnell   *Tues - Sats., May to September, or by appointment*
Tournaig, Poolewe   *By appointment: 01445 781250 or 781339*

ROXBURGH

Floors Castle, Kelso   *Daily Easter – end September 10am - 4.30pm,*
October: Sundays & Wednesdays 10am - 4pm

STEWARTRY OF KIRKCUDBRIGHT

Corsock House, Castle Douglas   *Open by appointment: 01644 440250*
Cally Gardens, Gatehouse of Fleet   *Sats & Suns, Easter to first weekend in October 10am - 5.30pm*

TWEEDDALE

Kailzie Gardens, Peebles   *Daily 22 March-18 October 11am-5.30pm*
Winter: Daylight hours, gardens only

WIGTOWN

Ardwell House Gardens, Ardwell   *Daily 28 March-30 September 10am-5pm*
Castle Kennedy & Lochinch Gardens   *Daily 28 March-30 September 10am-5pm*
Whitehills Garden & Nursery, Newton Stewart   *Daily 1 April - 31 October by appt: 01671 402049*

12

MONTHLY CALENDAR LIST

FEBRUARY

Date to be announced
Page

EDINBURGH & WEST LOTHIAN .... **DALMENY PARK,** South Queensferry 70

SUNDAY 9th FEBRUARY
RENFREW & INVERCLYDE .... **ARDGOWAN**, Inverkip 100

MARCH

SUNDAY 2nd MARCH
FIFE (provisionally) .... **CAMBO HOUSE,** Kingsbarns 76
STEWARTY OF KIRKCUDBRIGHT .... **DANEVALE PARK,** Crossmichael 112

TUESDAY 4th MARCH
MIDLOTHIAN .... **GREENFIELD LODGE,** Lasswade 90

SUNDAY 16th MARCH
CENTRAL .... **KILBRYDE CASTLE,** Dunblane 54
MIDLOTHIAN .... **PRESTONHALL,** Pathhead 92

TUESDAY 25th MARCH
MIDLOTHIAN .... **GREENFIELD LODGE,** Lasswade 90

APRIL

TUESDAY 1st APRIL
MIDLOTHIAN .... **GREENFIELD LODGE,** Lasswade 90

WEDNESDAY 2nd APRIL
ARGYLL .... **CNOC-NA-GARRIE,** by Lochgilphead 40

SUNDAY 6th APRIL
GLASGOW & DISTRICT .... **GREENBANK HOUSE & GARDEN,**
Clarkston 81

MAY

MONDAY 26th MAY

WEDNESDAY 28th MAY

SATURDAY 31st MAY

SATURDAY & SUNDAY 31st MAY & 1st JUNE

JUNE

SUNDAY 1st JUNE

TUESDAY 3rd JUNE

WEDNESDAY 4th JUNE

19

SUNDAY 6th JULY

TUESDAY 15th JULY

WEDNESDAY 16th JULY

SATURDAY & SUNDAY 19th & 20th JULY

SUNDAY 20th JULY

WEDNESDAY 23rd JULY

THURSDAY 24th JULY

SATURDAY & SUNDAY 26th & 27th JULY

SUNDAY 27th JULY

WEDNESDAY 30th JULY

AUGUST

SATURDAY 2nd AUGUST

SATURDAY & SUNDAY 2nd & 3rd AUGUST

SUNDAY 3rd AUGUST

OCTOBER

PLANT SALES in 1997

If any garden has a plant sale on the opening day this is mentioned in the text. The following Plant Sales are held as special events on their own and offer an opportunity to bring and buy. For further details see text.

Dunbartonshire West: THE HILL HOUSE, Helensburgh
Sunday 7th SEPTEMBER 11am - 5pm.

Glasgow & District: KILMARDINNY HOUSE ARTS CENTRE, Bearsden
Saturday 13 SEPTEMBER 11am - 4pm

Edinburgh & West Lothian: KIRKNEWTON HOUSE, Kirknewton
Saturday & Sunday 27th & 28th SEPTEMBER 11.30am - 4pm

Fife: HILL OF TARVIT, Cupar
Saturday 4th OCTOBER 10.30am - 4pm
Sunday 5th OCTOBER 2 - 5pm

Midlothian: OXENFOORD MAINS, Dalkeith
Sunday 12th OCTOBER 10.30am - 3pm

ABERDEEN

District Organiser	**Mrs David James Duff,** Hatton Castle, Turriff AB53 8ED
Area Organisers:	**Mrs W Bruce,** Logie House, Ellon AB41 8LH
	Mrs D M Crichton Maitland, Daluaine, Rhynie AB54 4HL
	Mrs F G Lawson, Asloun, Alford AB33 8NR
	Mrs A Robertson, Drumblade House, Huntly AB54 6ER
	Mrs F M K Tuck, Allargue House, Strathdon AB36 8YP
Hon. Treasurer:	**Mrs David James Duff**

DATES OF OPENING

23 Don Street, Old Aberdeen	April – September by appt.
Greenridge, Cults	July & August by appt.
Kirkstile House, Gartly	May - August by appt.
Nether Affloch Farmhouse, Dunecht	July & August by appt.
Old Semeil Herb Garden, Strathdon	May to August 10am - 5pm
Station Cottage, Gartly	June - August by appt.

Auchmacoy, Ellon	Sunday 20 April	1.30 – 4.30pm
Culquoich, Alford	Sunday 25 May	1.30 – 5pm
Kildrummy Castle Gardens, Alford	Sunday 1 June	10am – 5pm
Dunecht House Garden, Dunecht	Sunday 8 June	1 – 5pm
Dunecht House Garden, Dunecht	Sunday 15 June	1 – 5pm
Tertowie Garden, Clinterty	Sunday 15 June	1 – 4pm
Byth House, New Byth	Sunday 22 June	2 -5pm
Howemill, Craigievar, Alford	Sunday 22 June	1.30-5pm
Ploughman's Hall, Old Rayne	Sunday 29 June	1 - 6pm
Waterside Farmhouse, Oyne	Sunday 29 June	1 - 6pm
Ardmeallie, Bridge of Marnoch	Sunday 6 July	2 - 6pm
23 Don Street, Old Aberdeen	Sunday 13 July	1.30 – 6pm
Hatton Castle, Turriff	Sunday 13 July	1 - 5pm
Pitmedden Gardens, Pitmedden	Sunday 13 July	10 – 5.30pm
Leith Hall, Kennethmont, by Huntly	Sunday 20 July	1.30 – 5pm
Castle Fraser, Kemnay	Sunday 27 July	2 – 5pm
Esslemont, Ellon	Sunday 3 August	1 – 5pm
Haddo House, Tarves	Sunday 3 August	2 - 5pm
Dunecht House Garden, Dunecht	Sunday 24 August	1 - 5pm
Tillypronie, Tarland	Sunday 31 August	2 - 5pm

23 DON STREET, Old Aberdeen &

(Miss M Mackechnie)

A secret small walled garden in historic Old Aberdeen. Recently shown on 'The Beechgrove Garden'. Wide range of unusual plants and old-fashioned roses. Small pool with aquatic plants. Teas with home baking. Park at St Machar Cathedral, short walk down Chanonry to Don Street, turn right. City plan ref: P7.

Admission £1.50 Concessions £1.00

OPEN APRIL TO SEPTEMBER BY APPOINTMENT Tel: 01224 487269.

SUNDAY 13th JULY 1.30 – 6pm

40% to Cat Protection League

ARDMEALLIE, Bridge of Marnoch, Aberchirder &

(Mr & Mrs J Burnett-Stuart)

Mature garden with yew hedges, borders, shrubs, rose garden and fine views over Deveron valley. Teas. Plant stall. Route: Turn off Huntly/Banff road (A97) at Bridge of Marnoch (B9117) for one mile, signposts on the day.

Admission £1.50 Children 50p

SUNDAY 6th JULY 2 - 6pm

40% to St Marnan's Church, Aberchirder

AUCHMACOY, Ellon &

(Captain D W S Buchan)

Auchmacoy House policies feature an attractive display of tens of thousands of daffodils. Teas.

Admission £2.00 Children & OAPs £1.00

SUNDAY 20th APRIL 1.30 – 4.30 pm

40% to Gordon Highlanders Museum Appeal

BYTH HOUSE, New Byth, Turriff & partially

(Mr & Mrs A Windsor)

Herbaceous and shrub borders, herb gardens, kitchen garden. Woodland walk. Pond. Pony rides. Teas. Plant stall. New Byth is off A98.

Admission £1.50 Children & OAPs 50p

SUNDAY 22nd JUNE 2 - 5pm

40% to Riding for the Disabled (Banff & District branch)

CASTLE FRASER, Kemnay &

(The National Trust for Scotland)

Castle Fraser, one of the most spectacular of the Castles of Mar, belongs to the same period of native architectural achievements as Crathes Castle and Craigievar Castle. The walled garden has been fully restored by the Trust and forms a delightful adjunct to the Castle. Plant & vegetable sales. Tea room. Trails, pipe band, stalls, competitions, horse and carriage rides. Near Kemnay, off B993.

Admission £1.80 Children £1.20

SUNDAY 27th JULY 2 – 5 pm

40% to The Gardens Fund of The National Trust for Scotland

For other opening details see page 113

CULQUOICH, Alford
(Mrs M I Bell Tawse)
Natural woodlands, including an interesting pinetum, shrubs, spring bulbs, azaleas and rhododendrons. Tea and biscuits. Garden is west of Glenkindie village, opposite Glenkindie House, off main Alford-Strathdon road, A97.
Admission £1.00
SUNDAY 25th MAY 1.30 – 5 pm
40% to Arthritis and Rheumatism Council

DUNECHT HOUSE GARDENS, Dunecht   ♿ (partly)
(The Hon Charles A Pearson)
Romanesque addition, 1877, by G Edmund Street, to original House by John & William Smith. Herbaceous borders, heath and wild garden. Light refreshments. Cars free. Dunecht 1 mile. Routes A974, A944, B 977.
Admission £2.00 Children £1.00
SUNDAY 8th and SUNDAY 15th JUNE 1 – 5 pm
40% to Queen's Nursing Institute (Scotland)
SUNDAY 24th AUGUST 1 – 5 pm
40% to Aberdeen Branch Riding for the Disabled

ESSLEMONT, Ellon   ♿
(Mrs Robert Wolrige Gordon of Esslemont)
Victorian house set in wooded policies above River Ythan. Roses and shrubs in garden with double yew hedges (17th and 18th centuries). Music, stalls, charity stalls. Home baked teas. Ellon 2 miles. Take A920 from Ellon. On Pitmedden/Oldmeldrum road.
Admission: Cars £2.00
SUNDAY 3rd AUGUST 1 – 5 pm
15% to The Gordon Highlanders' Benevolent Trust, 15% to Marie Curie Cancer Care for North East Scotland, 10% between Tarves Boys' Brigade and St Mary on the Rock Graveyard.

GREENRIDGE, Craigton Road, Cults
(BP Exploration Co Ltd)
Large secluded garden surrounding 1840 Archibald Simpson house, for many years winner of Britain in Bloom 'Best Hidden Garden'. Mature specimen trees and shrubs. Sloping walled rose garden and terraces. Kitchen garden. Teas. Plant stall.
Admission £3.50 including tea
JULY and AUGUST by appointment. Tel: 01224 860200 Fax: 01224 860210
40% to Association of the Friends of Raeden

HADDO HOUSE, Tarves   ♿
(The National Trust for Scotland)
Attractive and prolific rose garden. Good herbaceous borders. Homebaked teas. Garden walks. Raffle. Musical entertainment. Off B999 4 miles north of Pitmedden, 19 miles north of Aberdeen.
Admission £1.50 Children free
SUNDAY 3rd AUGUST 2 - 5pm
40% to The Gardens Fund of the National Trust for Scotland

HATTON CASTLE, Turriff   ♿ with help
(Mr & Mrs James Duff)

Two acre walled garden with old fashioned shrub roses and herbaceous borders. Kitchen garden with fan trained fruit trees. Lake and woodland walks. Teas and homebaking. Good plant stall. Botanical paintings and presents. Pipe band and string quartet. On A947 2 miles south of Turriff.
Admission £2.00 Children free
SUNDAY 13th JULY 1 - 5pm
40% to Childrens Hospice Association Scotland

HOWEMILL, Craigievar   ♿ with help
(Mr D Atkinson)

Young garden with a wide range of unusual alpines, shrubs and herbaceous plants. Plant stall. Teas. From Alford take A980 Alford/Lumphanan road. No dogs please.
Admission £1.50 Children under 12 free
SUNDAY 22nd JUNE 1.30 - 5pm
40% to Cancer Relief Macmillan Fund

KILDRUMMY CASTLE GARDENS, Alford   ♿ (with help)
(Kildrummy Garden Trust)

April shows the gold of the lysichitons in the water garden, and the small bulbs naturalised beside the copy of the 14th century Brig o' Balgownie. Rhododendrons and azaleas from April (frost permitting). September/October brings colchicums and brilliant colour with acers, fothergillas and viburnums. Plants for sale. Play area. Video room. Wheelchair facilities. Car park free inside hotel main entrance. Coach park up hotel delivery entrance. Parties by arrangement. Open daily April - October.
Tel: 01975 571277/571203. On A97, 10 miles from Alford, 17 miles from Huntly.
Admission £1.70 Children 6 – 16 50p
SUNDAY 1st JUNE 10 am – 5 pm
20% to Queen's Nursing Institute (Scotland) and 20% to Fabric Fund, Kildrummy Church.

KIRKSTILE HOUSE, Gartly   ♿
(Mr & Mrs R Avis)

Three acre mature garden surrounding 18th century former manse. Many trees, shrubs, herbaceous borders, walled garden. Teas. Plant stall. No dogs please. 3 miles south of Huntly off A97 towards Rhynie, or follow Gartly signs from A96.
Admission £1.50 Children free
MAY to AUGUST by appointment. Tel: 01466 720243
40% to Wellbeing (The Health Research Charity for Women & Babies)

LEITH HALL, Kennethmont
(The National Trust for Scotland)
Quadrangular harled mansion dating from 1650. Home of Leith and Leith-Hay family until 1945. Public rooms contain interesting furniture, personal possessions and mementoes. The house tour incorporates all of the first floor, including the splendid oval room and a military collection on second floor. Garden contains a rock garden and zig-zag herbaceous and catmint borders. Chinese moon gate and Pictish stones. Extensive grounds with 18th century stables, ponds, including one with a bird observation hide, three countryside walks with one to a viewpoint overlooking surrounding countryside. Teas. Pipe band. On B9002 near Kennethmont.
Admission £1.80 Children & OAPs £1.20
SUNDAY 20th JULY 1.30 – 5pm
40% to The Gardens Fund of The National Trust for Scotland
For details of other openings see page 130

NETHER AFFLOCH FARMHOUSE, Dunecht   ㄴ (with help)
(Mr & Mrs M J Reid)
19th century renovated cottage garden with large collection of climbing roses. Fine views, mature trees, herbaceous borders. Unusual plants, many varieties of old fashioned and specie roses, herbs and alpines. Plants for sale. Groups very welcome. Sorry no dogs. Route A944.
Admission £2.00
JULY & AUGUST, by appointment. Tel. 01330 860362
40% to Ménière's Society

OLD SEMEIL HERB GARDEN, Strathdon   (partly)
(Mrs Gillian Cook)
Around 200 varieties of herb plants displayed growing in semi-formal display gardens. Established in 1981 in a sheltered site 1,000 feet above sea level. Specialist nursery, plant sales, tearoom and shop. Extra parking available. Access to patio, tearoom and toilets suitable for wheelchairs. Just off A944 Strathdon/Tomintoul, and 1¼ miles off A97 Huntly/Deeside in Strathdon. Tel: 01975 651343.
Admission by donation. SGS Collection Box.
MAY - AUGUST 10am - 5pm daily
40% to The Henry Doubleday Research Association

PITMEDDEN GARDEN, Ellon ㄴ
(The National Trust for Scotland)
Garden created by Lord Pitmedden in 1675. Recreated by the Trust from 1952, and is one of the very few gardens of this period in Scotland. Elaborate floral designs in parterres of box edging. Herbaceous borders, yew buttresses, pavilions, fountains and sundials. Also Museum of Farming Life, Visitor Centre, woodland walk. Tearoom. Special rates for pre-booked coach parties.
Admission £3.50 Concessions & children £2.30.
SUNDAY 13th JULY 10am – 5.30pm
40% to The Gardens Fund of The National Trust for Scotland
For details of other openings see page 131

PLOUGHMAN'S HALL, Old Rayne   ♿ with help
(Mr & Mrs A Gardiner)
One acre garden. Rock, herbaceous, kitchen, woodland and dried flower gardens.
Plant stall. Off A96, 9 miles north of Inverurie.
JOINT OPENING WITH WATERSIDE FARMHOUSE, OYNE
Admission £1.50 Children 50p
SUNDAY 29th JUNE 1 - 6pm
40% to Wycliffe Bible Translators

STATION COTTAGE, Gartly
(Travers & Betty Cosgrove)
Century old quarry converted into a "secret garden" by generations of railwaymen. Old
cottage plants. Climbing pathways through wild garden. Railway site preserved. Plants
for sale. Railway still in use. 5 miles south of Huntly on A97 towards Rhynie. Follow
signs for Gartly from A96.
Admission £1.00 Children & OAPs 50p
JUNE to AUGUST by appointment. Tel: 01466 720277
40% to Parish of Noth, Church of Scotland

TERTOWIE, Clinterty   ♿
(Aberdeen College)
Half acre walled garden with established herbaceous and mixed borders. A new rose
garden and seaside garden have recently been added along with new mixed borders.
4 acres of grounds set in mature woodland with shade garden, peat garden & extensive
streamside plantings. Many new and unusal varieties of plants as well as the National
Collection of Rubus. Woodland walks through surrounding area. Teas. Plant stall.
Dogs on lead please. Follow signs for Clinterty from A96 Aberdeen/Inverness,
Tertowie signposted at next junction. From A944 Aberdeen/Alford signposted after
5 mile garage.
Admission £1.50 Concessions 75p
SUNDAY 15th JUNE 1 - 4pm
40% to Aberdeen Disabled Persons Trust

TILLYPRONIE, Tarland ♿
(The Hon Philip Astor)
Late Victorian house. Herbaceous borders, terraced garden with pond at bottom.
Shrubs, heaths and ornamental trees in pinetum. Vegetable garden. Superb views.
Picnic area. Free car park. Dogs on lead, please. Teas.
Admission £1.50 Children 75p
SUNDAY 31st AUGUST 2 – 5 pm
All proceeds to Scotland's Gardens Scheme

 # WATERSIDE FARMHOUSE, Oyne
(Ann & Colin Millar)
A developing garden, started in 1991 from a rough farmyard. Recently planted
woodland extends to 2 acres around 19th century farmhouse and courtyard with
cordoned fruit trees and kitchen garden. Mixed shrub and herbaceous borders, pond,
heathers and herbs. Teas. No dogs please. Off A96, ½ mile north of junction with B9002.
JOINT OPENING WITH PLOUGHMAN'S HALL, OLD RAYNE
Admission £1.50 Children 50p
SUNDAY 29th JUNE 1 - 6pm
40% to Books Abroad

ANGUS

District Organiser:	**Mrs Jonathan Stansfeld**, Dunninald, by Montrose DD10 9TD
Area Organisers:	**Miss Ruth Dundas**, Caddam, Kinnordy, Kirriemuir DD8 4LP
	Mrs R Ephraums, Damside, Leysmill, Arbroath DD11 4RS
	Mrs A Houstoun, Kerbet House, Kinnettles, Forfar DD8 1TQ
	Mrs R H V Learoyd, Priestoun, Edzell DD9 7UD
	Mrs T D Lloyd-Jones, Reswallie House, by Forfar DD8 2SA
Hon. Treasurer:	**Col R H B Learoyd**, Priestoun, Edzell DD9 7UD

DATES OF OPENING

House of Pitmuies, Guthrie, by Forfar .... Easter to 31 October   10am-5pm

Brechin Castle, Brechin	Sunday 25 May	2-5.30pm
Cortachy Castle, Kirriemuir	Sunday 1 June	2 - 6pm
Kinnettles House, by Forfar	Sunday 8 June	2 - 6pm
Dunninald, Montrose	Sunday 22 June	2 - 5.30pm
House of Dun, Montrose	Saturday 28 June	12.30-5pm
Brechin Castle, Brechin	Sunday 6 July	2-5.30pm
Glamis Castle	Sunday 6 July	10am-5.30pm
Edzell Village & Edzell Castle	Sunday 27 July	1.30-5.30pm
Kinpurnie Castle, Newtyle	Sunday 3 August	2 - 6pm
Bannatyne House, Newtyle	Sunday 10 August	1.30 - 6pm
Newtyle Village	Sunday 10 August	1.30 - 6pm

BANNATYNE HOUSE, Newtyle   ♿ (with help)
(Sir Gregor & Lady MacGregor of MacGregor)
Sixteenth century tower house with late additions. Shrub and herbaceous garden.
House not open. Teas at Newtyle Church Hall. On B954 between Meigle and Dundee.
JOINT OPENING WITH NEWTYLE VILLAGE
Admission includes all gardens: £2.00 Children under 12 free
SUNDAY 10th AUGUST 1.30 - 6pm
20% to Riding for the Disabled   20% to Scottish Masonic Homes Fund

---

BRECHIN CASTLE, Brechin
(The Earl & Countess of Dalhousie)
Ancient fortress of Scottish kings on cliff overlooking River Southesk. Rebuilt by
Alexander Edward - completed in 1711. Extensive walled garden half a mile from
Castle with ancient and new plantings and mown lawn approach. Rhododendrons,
azaleas, bulbs, interesting trees, wild garden. Tea in garden. Car parking free.
Route A90.
Admission £1.50 Children 50p
SUNDAY 25th MAY and SUNDAY 6th July 2 - 5.30pm
15% to RSSPC, 15% to Save the Children Fund, 10% to NCCPG

CORTACHY CASTLE, Kirriemuir
(The Earl & Countess of Airlie)
16th century castellated house. Additions in 1872 by David Bryce. Spring garden and
wild pond garden with azaleas, primroses and rhododendrons. Garden of fine
American specie trees and river walk along South Esk. Teas. Garden quiz.
Kirriemuir 5 miles. Route B955.
Admission £1.75 Children 25p
SUNDAY 1st JUNE 2 - 6 pm
40% to Cortachy Church

DUNNINALD, Montrose   ♿
(Mr & Mrs Stansfeld)
Traditional walled garden with mixed borders, vegetables, fruit trees, greenhouse.
Extensive grounds and beech avenue. Castle built in 1823 by James Gillespie Graham.
Teas. Plant stall. Route: 2 miles south of Montrose off A92, off Lunan/Montrose road.
Admission £1.50 Children 50p
SUNDAY 22nd JUNE 2 - 5.30pm
20% to YMCA Montrose   20% to Multiple Sclerosis Society

EDZELL VILLAGE & EDZELL CASTLE
Walk round 12 or 13 gardens in Edzell village. Edzell Castle is also on view. Teas extra.
Tickets are on sale in the village and a plan is issued with the tickets. Piper. Plant stall.
Admission £2.00 Children 50p
SUNDAY 27th JULY 1.30 - 5.30 pm
40% to Cancer Relief Macmillan Fund

GLAMIS CASTLE, Glamis ♿
(The Earl & Countess of Strathmore & Kinghorne)
Family home of the Earls of Strathmore and a royal residence since 1372. Childhood
home of HM Queen Elizabeth The Queen Mother, birthplace of HRH The Princess
Margaret, and legendary setting for Shakespeare's play 'Macbeth'. Five-storey L-shaped
tower block dating from 15th century, remodelled 1600, containing magnificent rooms
with wide range of historic pictures, furniture, porcelain etc. Spacious grounds with
river and woodland paths. Nature trail. Impressive policy timbers. Formal garden.
Restaurant. Teas. Four gift shops. Glamis 1 mile A94.
Admission to Castle & grounds: £5.00, OAPs £3.80, children £2.60.
Admission: Grounds only £2.30 Children & OAPs £1.20
SUNDAY 6th JULY 10am - 5.30pm
40% to Action Research

HOUSE OF DUN, Montrose ♿
(The National Trust for Scotland)
A fine Georgian house overlooking Montrose Basin, designed and built by William
Adam in 1730 for David Erskine, Lord Dun, containing fine furnishing and superb
plasterwork by Joseph Enzer. Attractive grounds with magnificent parkland trees and
woodland walks. The walled garden has been largely restored to a late Victorian period
and includes a range of plants typical of the 1880s. Handloom weavers' workshop.
Plant stall. Tearoom. Off A935 4m west of Montrose.
Admission to House & Garden: £3.50 Concessions £2.30 Family Group £9.30
Garden & grounds only £1.00
SATURDAY 28th JUNE 12.30pm - 5pm
40% to The Gardens Fund of The National Trust for Scotland

HOUSE OF PITMUIES, Guthrie, By Forfar

(Mrs Farquhar Ogilvie)

Semi-formal old walled gardens adjoining 18th century house. Massed spring bulbs, roses, herbaceous borders and a wide variety of shrubs. Old fashioned roses in summer with long borders of herbaceous perennials and superb delphiniums. Riverside walk with fine trees, interesting turreted doocot and "Gothic" wash-house. Dogs on lead please. Rare & unusual plants for sale. Fruit in season. Friockheim 1½ m Route A932. Admission £2.00

EASTER to 31st OCTOBER 10 am - 5 pm

Donation to Scotland's Gardens Scheme

KINNETTLES HOUSE, Douglastown, by Forfar

(Mr & Mrs Hugh Walker-Munro)

Rhododendron walk and rare trees and a mausoleum where an Indian princess is said to be buried. Formal terraced garden. Three miles south of Forfar on A94. Signed from main road or Dundee/Forfar road, 8 miles. Follow signs for Douglastown. Admission £1.50 Children free

SUNDAY 8th JUNE 2 - 6pm

40% to Kirriemuir Day Centre

KINPURNIE CASTLE, Newtyle

(Sir James Cayzer Bt)

Early 20th century house (not open). Panoramic views of the vale of Strathmore and the Grampians. Shrubs and herbaceous garden. The Ladies Palm Court Orchestra will play. Route B954. Dundee 10 m. Perth 18 m. Admission £1.50 Children 25p

SUNDAY 3rd AUGUST 2 - 6 pm

40% to Angus branch, British Red Cross

NEWTYLE VILLAGE   ♿ (with assistance)

Several cottage gardens, planted in a variety of styles, may be visited in the course of a short walk round the village of Newtyle. The village, with its regular street plan, was laid out in 1832 next to the northern terminus of Scotland's first passenger railway.

Tickets on sale at the Church Hall. Plants for sale. Teas in Church Hall. Newtyle is on B954 between Meigle and Dundee, 2 miles off A94 between Coupar Angus and Glamis.

JOINT OPENING WITH BANNATYNE HOUSE

Admission includes all gardens and tea: £2.00 Children under 12 free

SUNDAY 10th AUGUST 1.30 - 6pm

20% to Riding for the Disabled
20% to Scottish Masonic Homes Fund

ARGYLL

District Organiser **Lt Cmdr H D Campbell-Gibson,** Tighnamara, Melfort,
& Hon Treasurer   Kilmelford PA34 4XD

Area Organisers: **Miss Diana Crosland,** Maam, Glen Shira,
            Inveraray PA32 8XH
            Mrs Charles Gore, Port Namine, Taynuilt PA35 1HU

DATES OF OPENING

Achnacloich, Connel	Daily 24 March-31 October	10am – 6pm
An Cala, Ellenabeich	Daily 1 April-15 October	10am – 6pm
Appin House, Appin	Daily 14 April- 12 October	10am - 6pm
Ardanaiseig Hotel Gardens	Daily all year	9am - 5pm
Ardchattan Priory, North Connel.	Daily 1 April-30 October	9am – 6pm
Ardkinglas Woodland Garden	Open all year	
Ardmaddy Castle, Balvicar	Daily all year or by appt.	
Barguillean's 'Angus Garden'Taynuilt ..	Open all year	
Cnoc-na-Garrie, Ballymeanoch	By appointment	
Coille Dharaich, Kilmelford	By appointment	
Crarae Glen Garden, Inveraray	Daily April-October	9am – 6pm
Crinan Hotel Garden, Crinan	Daily 30 April to 30 September	
Dalnaheish, Tayvallich .	April-September by appointment	
Druimavuic House, Appin	Daily 13 April - 29th June	10am – 6pm
Druimneil House, Port Appin	Daily 28 March-19 June	9am – 6pm
Eredine Woodland Garden, Lochaweside	Saturdays all year, except 14 June	11am - 4pm
Glenfeochan House Hotel, Kilmore	Daily 15 March-31 October	10am – 6pm
Jura House, Ardfin, Isle of Jura.	Open all year	9am – 5pm
Kildalloig, Campbeltown	By appointment	
Kinlochlaich House Gardens, Appin. ...	Open all year (except Sundays Oct-Mar) 9.30–5.30 or dusk. Suns April-Sept 10.30-5.30.	
Mount Stuart, Rothesay, Isle of Bute	2 May–12 October (not Tues & Thurs) House: 11–5pm Gardens: 10am-5pm.	
Tighnamara, Kilmelford	By appointment, Spring – Autumn	
Torosay Castle Gardens, Isle of Mull	Open all year Summer: 9am-7pm Winter: Sunrise – Sunset	

Cnoc-na-Garrie, Ballymeanoch	Wednesday 2 April	2 - 6pm
Mount Stuart House & Gardens, Isle of Bute	Sat&Sun 19/20 April	10am - 5pm
	Sat&Sun 26/27 April	10am - 5pm
Younger Botanic Garden, Benmore	Sunday 27 April	10am - 6pm
Crinan Hotel Garden, Crinan	Saturday 3 May	11am - 6pm
Cnoc-na-Garrie, Ballymeanoch	Wednesday 7 May	2 - 6pm

Arduaine, Kilmelford	Sat&Sun 10/11 May	9.30 – 6pm
Colintraive Gardens Weekend	Sat&Sun 17/18 May	2 – 6pm
Ardkinglas House, Cairndow	Sunday 18 May	11am – 5pm
Kyles of Bute Gardens	Sat&Sun 31 May/1 June	2 – 6pm
Lossit, Macrihanish	Sunday 1 June	2 - 6pm
Cnoc-na-Garrie, Ballymeanoch	Wednesday 4 June	2 – 6pm
Coille Dharaich, Kilmelford	Sat&Sun 14/15 June	2 – 6pm
Tighnamara, Melfort, Kilmelford	Sat&Sun 14/15 June	2 – 6pm
Cnoc-na-Garrie, Ballymeanoch	Wednesday 2 July	2 - 6pm
Ardchattan Priory Fete	Sunday 20 July	
Kildalloig, Campbeltown	Sunday 20 July	2 - 5.30pm
Ormsary, Lochgilphead	Sunday 27 July	2 – 6pm
Cnoc-na-Garrie, Ballymeanoch	Wednesday 6 August	2 - 6pm
Cnoc-na-Garrie, Ballymeanoch	Wednesday 3 September	2 - 6pm

ACHNACLOICH, Connel &

(Mrs T E Nelson)
Scottish baronial house by John Starforth of Glasgow. Succession of bulbs, flowering shrubs, rhododendrons, azaleas and primulas. Woodland garden above Loch Etive. Plants for sale. Admission by collecting box. Dogs on lead please. On the A85 3miles east of Connel.
Admission £1.50   Children free OAPs £1.00
Daily from 24th MARCH to 31st OCTOBER 10am - 6pm
40% between Queen's Nursing Institute (Scotland) and the Gardens Fund of The National Trust for Scotland

---

AN CALA, Ellenabeich, Isle of Seil

(Mr & Mrs Thomas Downie)
A small garden of under five acres designed in the 1930s, An Cala sits snugly in its horse-shoe shelter of surrounding cliffs. A very pretty garden with streams, waterfall, ponds, many herbaceous plants as well as azaleas, rhododendrons and cherry trees in spring. Proceed south from Oban on Campbeltown road for 8 miles, turn right at Easdale sign, a further 8 miles on B844; garden between school and Inshaig Park Hotel.
Admission £1.00 Children free
Daily from 1st APRIL to 15th OCTOBER 10am - 6pm
Donation to Scotland's Gardens Scheme and Red Cross

APPIN HOUSE, Appin

(Mr & Mrs D Mathieson)
In an elevated position, overlooking the Lynn of Lorne and the islands of Shuna, Lismore and Mull, Appin House has magnificent views. The garden was initially planted in the 1960s. It contains many interesting trees and shrubs, as well as peaceful water features, colourful terraces and borders, and plentiful spring bulbs. The many azaleas make spring time walks particularly fragrant. Dogs on lead please. Plant stall. Off A828 midway between Oban and Fort William. Bus will stop at foot of road.
Admission £1.50   Children free   OAPs £1.00
DAILY 14th APRIL to 12th OCTOBER 10am - 6pm
Donation to Scotland's Gardens Scheme

ARDANAISEIG HOTEL GARDENS, Lochaweside
(Mr Bennie Gray)

Beautifully situated on Lochaweside, Ardanaiseig Country House Hotel is surrounded by some 100 acres of gardens, forest and woodland walks. Primarily a spring garden and originally laid out in the 1820s, there are many varieties of rhododendrons, azaleas, magnolias and other exotic shrubs and specimen trees. An extensive walled garden which has been rather neglected in recent years is hopefully being restored to its former standard. Teas. Plant stall. 21 miles from Oban. A85 to junction with B845, follow to Kilchrenan Inn, left to Ardanaiseig.

Admission £2.00 Children 50p

OPEN ALL YEAR 9am - 5pm

Donation to Scotland's Gardens Scheme

ARDCHATTAN PRIORY, North Connel &
(Mrs Sarah Troughton)

Beautifully situated on the north side of Loch Etive. The Priory, founded in 1230, is now a private house. The ruins of the chapel and graveyard, with fine early stones, are in the care of Historic Scotland and open with the garden. The front of the house has a rockery, formal herbaceous and rose borders, with excellent views over Loch Etive. To the west of the house there are shrub borders and a wild garden, numerous roses and over 30 different varieties of Sorbus providing excellent autumn colour. Oban 10 miles. From north, turn left off A828 at Barcaldine on to B845 for 6 miles. From Oban or the east on A85, cross Connel Bridge and turn first right, proceed east on Bonawe road. Tea and light lunches 11am - 6pm (April-Sept)

Admission £1.00 Children free

Daily from 1st APRIL to 30th OCTOBER 9am - 6pm.

A fete will be held on **SUNDAY 20th JULY**

Donation to Scotland's Gardens Scheme

ARDKINGLAS HOUSE, Cairndow &
(Mr S J Noble)

Set around Ardkinglas House, Robert Lorimer's favourite work, the informal garden of around five acres contains magnificent azaleas, trees and other shrubs. The "Caspian", a large pool, enhances the garden's beauty. Teas, coffee, soft drinks and home baking. Plant stall. Adjacent to Ardkinglas Woodland Gardens. Turn into Cairndow village from A83 Glasgow/Campbeltown road. Enter Ardkinglas estate through iron gates and follow sign.

Admission £1.50 Children free

SUNDAY 18th MAY 11 am - 5 pm

40% to Ardkinglas Arts Trust

ARDKINGLAS WOODLAND GARDEN, Cairndow & (partly)
(Ardkinglas Estate)

This garden contains one of Britain's finest collections of conifers, including "Europe's Mightiest Conifer" and a spectacular display of rhododendrons. Presently, it is undergoing extensive renovation with many improvements already made. It is hoped that visitors will be interested in seeing the garden develop over the coming years. Picnic facilities. Dogs allowed on lead. Entrance through Cairndow village off A83.

Admission £2.00

OPEN DAILY ALL YEAR ROUND

Donation to Scotland's Gardens Scheme

ARDMADDY CASTLE, Balvicar, by Oban ♿ (mostly)
(Mr & Mrs Charles Struthers)

Ardmaddy Castle, with its woodlands and formal walled garden on one side and extended views to the islands and the sea on the other, has some fine rhododendrons and azaleas with a variety of trees, shrubs, unusual vegetables and flower borders between dwarf box hedges. Woodland walks, recently created water garden. Plant stall with some unusual varieties, vegetables when available. Oban 13 miles, Easdale 3 miles. 1½ miles of narrow road off B844 to Easdale.

Admission £2.00 Children 50p

DAILY ALL YEAR

Other visits by arrangement: Tel. 01852 300353

Donations to Scotland's Gardens Scheme

ARDUAINE, Kilmelford
(The National Trust for Scotland)

Remarkable coastal garden on a hillside overlooking Loch Melfort and the Sound of Jura. Its internationally famous collection of rhododendron species is mainly sheltered within a Japanese larch woodland while, below, the water garden provides an informal setting for a wide range of trees, shrubs and perennials which thrive in the mild climate of the western seaboard. Located between Oban and Lochgilphead on the A816, sharing an entrance with the Loch Melfort Hotel.

Admission £2.30 Children & OAPs £1.50

SATURDAY & SUNDAY 10th & 11th MAY 9.30 am - 6 pm

40% to The Gardens Fund of The National Trust for Scotland

For other opening details see page 112

BARGUILLEAN'S "ANGUS GARDEN", Taynuilt
(Mr Sam Macdonald)

Nine acre woodland garden around eleven acre loch set in the Glen Lonan hills. Spring flowering bulbs, extensive collection of rhododendron hybrids, deciduous azaleas, shrubs, primulas and conifers. Garden recently extended by two acres. Access and car park provided. The garden contains the largest collection of North American rhododendron hybrids in the west of Scotland. Coach tours by arrangement: Tel: 01866 822333 or Fax: 01866 822375. Taynuilt 3 miles.

Admission £2.00 Children free

DAILY ALL YEAR

Donation to Scotland's Gardens Scheme

CNOC-NA-GARRIE, Ballymeanoch, by Lochgilphead
(Mrs Dorothy Thomson)

A garden being created from rough hillside, designed for year-round interest. Large range of alpines, shrubs, grasses, herbaceous plants and bulbs, many grown from seed. Plant stall. 2m south of Kilmartin, A816. Entrance sharp left between cottages and red brick house, continue up track to bungalow.

Admission £1.00 Accompanied children free.

Wednesdays 2nd APRIL, 7th MAY, 4th JUNE, 2nd JULY, 6th AUG., 3rd SEPT. 2-6pm
(or by arrangement.) Tel: 01546 605327.

20% to British Red Cross Society (mid Argyll)   20% to Cancer Relief Macmillan Fund

COILLE DHARAICH, Kilmelford, Oban &

(Drs Alan & Hilary Hill)
Small garden, centred on natural rock outcrop, pool and scree terraces and troughs.
Wide variety of primulas, alpines, dwarf conifers, bulbs, bog and peat loving plants.
No dogs please. Plant stall. Half a mile from Kilmelford on road signposted "Degnish".
Admission £1.00 Children free
SATURDAY & SUNDAY 14th & 15th JUNE 2 - 6 pm
Other days by arrangement. Tel: 01852 200285
40% to North Argyll Eventide Home Association

COLINTRAIVE GARDENS

Three delightful spring and woodland gardens of varied interest, within easy reach of
each other. Set in a scenic corner of Argyll.

1 - **Stronailne**	Mr & Mrs H Andrew
2 - **Dunyvaig**	Mrs M Donald
3 - **Tigh-na-beag**	Mr & Mrs J W Morris

Please call at No. 1 for admission tickets and directions. Dogs on lead please. Plant stall.
On A886, 20 miles from Dunoon.
Admission £1.50 Children 50p includes all gardens
SATURDAY & SUNDAY 17th and 18th MAY 2 - 6 pm
All takings to Scotland's Gardens Scheme

CRARAE, Inveraray & (only Lower Gardens)

(Crarae Gardens Charitable Trust)
Rhododendrons, exotic trees and shrubs in a highland glen.
Spectacular spring and autumn colour. Dogs on short lead please. Plant sales and
Visitor Centre open 10 am - 5 pm April to October. Minard 1 mile. 11 miles south of
Inveraray on A83.
Admission: Fixed charge. Car Parking & Children under 5 free
Daily APRIL to OCTOBER 9am - 6pm
Donation to Scotland's Gardens Scheme

CRINAN HOTEL GARDEN, Crinan

(Mr & Mrs N Ryan)
Rock garden with azaleas and rhododendrons created into the hillside over a century
ago and sheltered, secluded garden with sloping lawns, unexpected herbaceous beds
and spectacular views of the canal and Crinan Loch. Lochgilphead A83. A816 Oban,
then A841 Cairnbaan to Crinan. Collecting box.
End APRIL to end SEPTEMBER daily
Special Open Day SATURDAY 3rd MAY 11am - 6pm Plant stall. Teas.
Admission £1.50 Accompanied children free
40% to Mid Argyll Hospital

DALNAHEISH, Tayvallich

(Mrs C J Lambie)
Small, informal old garden overlooking the Sound of Jura. Woodland, planted rock,
shrubs, bulbs, rhododendrons, azaleas and a wide variety of plants from around the
world. Donations. One mile from Tayvallich.
Admission by telephone appointment: Tel. 01546 870286
APRIL to SEPTEMBER
All takings to Scotland's Gardens Scheme

DRUIMAVUIC HOUSE, Appin

(Mr & Mrs Newman Burberry)

Stream, wall and woodland gardens with lovely views over Loch Creran. Spring bulbs, rhododendrons, azaleas, primulas, meconopsis, violas. Dogs on lead please. Plant stall. Route A828 Oban/Fort William, 4 miles south of Appin. Use private road where public signs warn of flooding.

Admission £1.00 Children free

Daily from 13th APRIL to 29th JUNE 10 am - 6 pm

Donation to Scotland's Gardens Scheme

DRUIMNEIL HOUSE, Port Appin

(Mrs J Glaisher & Mr Allan Paterson)

Ten acre garden overlooking Loch Linnhe with many fine varieties of mature trees and rhododendrons and other woodland shrubs. Home made teas available. Collection box. 2 miles from A828. Connel/Fort William road. Sharp left at Airds Hotel, second house on right. Lunches by prior arrangement. Tel: 01631 730228.

Admission 50p Children free

Daily from 28th MARCH to 19th JUNE 9am - 6pm

All takings to Scotland's Gardens Scheme

EREDINE WOODLAND GARDEN, Lochaweside

(Dr & Mrs K Goel)

Woodland garden of 29 acres consisting of attractive mature trees with abundance of wild flowers. Rhododendrons, azaleas, cherry trees and many others. Massed snowdrops followed by daffodils and bluebells. Woodland and lochside walks with spectacular views. On B840. Ford 8m, Dalmally 20m, Inveraray 23m.

Admission £1.00 Children & OAPs 50p. All children under the age of 12 years must be accompanied by an adult. No pets allowed (except guide dogs).

OPEN SATURDAYS ALL YEAR (except 14th June) 11am - 4pm

Donation to Scotland's Gardens Scheme

GLENFEOCHAN HOUSE HOTEL, Kilmore, by Oban

(Mr & Mrs D Baber)

Over 100 different rhododendrons. Azaleas, specimen trees and tender flowering shrubs. Carpets of spring bulbs and beautiful autumn colours. Walled garden with herbaceous border, herbs, fruit and vegetables. Plant stall. Teas. Produce when available. 5 miles south of Oban at head of Loch Feochan on A816.

Admission £2.00 Children 50p

Daily from 15th MARCH to 31st OCTOBER 10 am - 6 pm

Donation to Scotland's Gardens Scheme

JURA HOUSE, Ardfin, Isle of Jura

(Mr F A Riley-Smith)

Organic walled garden with wide variety of unusual plants and shrubs, including large Australasian collection. Also interesting woodland and cliff walk, spectacular views. Points of historical interest, abundant wild life and flowers. Plant stall. Tea tent in season. Toilet. 5 miles from ferry terminal. Ferries to Islay from Kennacraig by Tarbert.

Admission £2.00 Students £1.00 Children up to 16 free

OPEN ALL YEAR 9 am - 5 pm

Donation to Scotland's Gardens Scheme

KILDALLOIG, Campbeltown ♿ (partially)
(Mr & Mrs Joe Turner)
Coastal garden with some interesting and unusual shrubs and herbaceous perennials.
Woodland walk. Pond area under construction. Teas. Plant stall. Dogs on lead please.
3 miles south of Campbeltown past Davaar Island.
Admission £1.50 Accompanied children free.
SUNDAY 20th JULY 2 - 5.30pm or by appointment. Tel: 01586 553192.
40% to Royal National Lifeboat Institution

KINLOCHLAICH HOUSE GARDENS, Appin ♿ (Gravel paths sloping)
(Mr D E Hutchison)
Closed Sundays mid October - March. Walled garden, incorporating the West
Highlands' largest Nursery Garden Centre. Display beds of alpines, heathers, primulas,
rhododendrons, azaleas and herbaceous plants. Fruiting and flowering shrubs and
trees. Route A828. Oban 23 miles, Fort William 27 miles. Bus stops at gate by Police
Station.
Admission £1.00
OPEN DAILY ALL YEAR 9.30am - 5.30pm or dusk except Sundays October to March.
(Sundays April - Sept. 10.30am - 5.30pm)
Donation to Scotland's Gardens Scheme

KYLES OF BUTE SMALL GARDENS, Tighnabruaich
Four small gardens in and around Tighnabruaich within easy reach of each other. Each
garden entirely different with something of interest for everyone. Plant sale. Dogs on
lead please.

1 - **Alt Mhor,** Auchenlochan	Mr & Mrs Peter Scott
2 - **The Cottage,** Tighnabruich	Col. & Mrs Peter Halliday
3 - **Rhubaan Lodge,** Tighnabruich	Mr & Mrs R M Scott
4 - **Heatherfield,** Kames	Mr & Mrs David Johnston

Please call at No.1 first for admission tickets and directions.
Admission £1.50 Children 50p, includes all 4 gardens
SATURDAY & SUNDAY 31st MAY & 1st JUNE 2 - 6 pm
All takings to Scotland's Gardens Scheme

LOSSIT, Machrihanish
(Mr & Mrs Hector Macneal)
Rhododendrons, azaleas, many shrubs, semi-tropical plants. Sunken kitchen garden.
Attractive woodland walk and sea views to Islay, Jura, Gigha and Northern Ireland.
Dogs on lead, please. Tea in garage. Three quarters of a mile from Machrihanish. Bus:
Campbeltown to Machrihanish.
Admission £1.50 Accompanied children free.
SUNDAY 1st JUNE 2 - 6pm
40% to British Red Cross (Campbeltown branch)

MOUNT STUART HOUSE & GARDENS, Rothesay, Isle of Bute &

(Mount Stuart Trust)

Open to the public for the first time in 1995: ancestral home of the Marquesses of Bute; one of Britain's most spectacular High Victorian Gothic houses, set in 300 acres. Fabulous interiors, art collection and architectural detail; extensive grounds with lovely woodland and shoreline walks; exotic gardens, Victorian kitchen garden; mature Victorian pinetum. Tearoom & picnic areas. Pre-booked house/gardens/ranger guided tours available on application. Admission to House & Garden: £5.50 Child £2.50 Family ticket £15. Concessions and group rates given.

Admission to Garden only: £3 Child £2 Family ticket £8

House: 11am - 5pm Gardens: 10am - 5pm (Last admission to both 4.30pm)

Gardens open **Saturday & Sunday 19th & 20th and 26th & 27th APRIL and 2nd MAY to 12th OCTOBER incl.** Closed Tuesdays and Thursdays. Sorry no dogs.

Donation to Scotland's Gardens Scheme

ORMSARY, by Lochgilphead &

(Sir William & Lady Lithgow)

Small walled garden, wild shrub garden, woodland walks to waterfall. Veteran car rides. Plant stall. Home baked teas under cover. South of Ardrishaig, take Kilberry road B8024. 10 miles to Ormsary from turn-off on A83.

Admission £1.60 Children & OAPs 70p

SUNDAY 27th JULY 2 - 6pm

20% to South Knapdale Parish Church   20% to Mid Argyll Voluntary Transport Group

---

TIGHNAMARA, Melfort, Kilmelford

(Lt Cmdr & Mrs H D Campbell-Gibson)

Two acre garden set in an ancient oak wood with outstanding views over Loch Melfort. Interesting variety of shrubs and many perennial plants. Paths with terraced beds up hillside. Woodland garden with pool, surrounded by massed primulas, hostas, cranesbill geraniums and astilbes and an abundance of bulbs and wild flowers. Teas. Plant stall. One mile from Kilmelford on lochside road to Degnish.

Amission £1.00 Accompanied children free

SATURDAY & SUNDAY 14th & 15th JUNE 2 - 6pm

By appointment any day between Spring and Autumn. Tel: 01852 200224.

40% to World Society for the Protection of Animals

TOROSAY CASTLE & GARDENS, Isle of Mull

(Mr Christopher James)

Torosay is a beautiful and welcoming family home completed in 1858 by David Bryce in the Scottish Baronial style and is surrounded by 12 acres of spectacular contrasting gardens which include formal terraces, an impressive Italian statue walk, surrounded by varied woodland. Tearoom. Craft shop. Free parking. Groups welcome. 1½ miles from Craignure. Miniature rail steam/diesel from Craignure. Regular daily ferry service from Oban to Craignure.

Admission to Castle & Gardens £4.50 Children £1.50 Concessions £3.50

Castle open Easter weekend - mid October 10.30am - 5.30pm

GARDENS OPEN ALL YEAR Summer 9am - 7pm; Winter sunrise - sunset, with reduced admission when Castle closed.

Donation to Scotland's Gardens Scheme

YOUNGER BOTANIC GARDEN   ♿ (limited due to hill slopes)
(Specialist Garden of the Royal Botanic Garden, Edinburgh)
World famous for its magnificent conifers and its extensive range of flowering trees and shrubs, including over 250 species of rhododendron. From a spectacular avenue of Giant Redwoods, numerous waymarked walks lead the visitor via a formal garden and pond through hillside woodlands to a dramatic viewpoint overlooking the Eachaig valley and the Holy Loch. Free guided tours of spring colour throughout the open day. James Duncan Cafe (licensed) and Botanics Shop for gifts and plants. Dogs permitted on a short leash. 7m north of Dunoon or 22m south from Glen Kinglass below Rest and Be Thankful pass; on A815.
Admission £2.00 Concessions £1.50 Children 50p Families £4.50
SUNDAY 27th APRIL   10am - 6pm
40% to Royal Botanic Garden, Edinburgh

AYRSHIRE

District Organiser:	**The Countess of Lindsey**, Gilmilnscroft, Sorn, Mauchline KA5 6ND
Area Organisers:	**Mrs R F Cuninghame,** Caprington Castle, Kilmarnock KA2 9AA
	Mrs John Greenall, Lagg House, Dunure KA7 4LE
	Mrs R Y Henderson, Blairston, by Ayr KA7 4EF
	Mrs R M Yeomans, Ashcraig, Skelmorlie PA17 5HB
Hon. Treasurer:	**Mrs Edith Kerr,** Bank of Scotland, 123 High Street, Ayr KA7 1QP

DATES OF OPENING

Bargany, Girvan .... 1 March - 31 Oct   10am - 7pm or dusk
Blair, Dalry .... All year round

Culzean Castle & Country Park .... Sunday 13 April   10.30am – 5pm
Culzean Castle & Country Park .... Sunday 4 May   10.30am – 5pm
Auchincruive, Ayr .... Sunday 18 May   1 – 5.30pm
Barnweil, Craigie, nr Kilmarnock .... Sunday 8 June   2 – 5pm
Fairlie Gardens .... Saturday 14 June   2 - 5pm
Martnaham Lodge, by Ayr .... Sunday 15 June   2 - 5pm
Penkill Castle, near Girvan .... Sunday 29 June   2 - 5pm
Culzean Castle & Country Park .... Thursday 10 July   10.30am – 5pm
Kingencleuch, Mauchline .... Sunday 13 July   2 - 5.30pm
Carnell, Hurlford .... Sunday 27 July   2 – 5.30pm
Skeldon, Dalrymple .... Sunday 3 August   2 – 6pm
Bardrochat, Colmonell .... Sunday 10 August   2 - 5.30pm
Blairquhan, Straiton, Maybole .... Sunday 17 August   1.30 – 4.30pm

AUCHINCRUIVE, Ayr
(Scottish Agricultural College)

Extensive amenity grounds of the College campus, the setting for buildings and other facilities serving all aspects of the educational, research and consultancy work of the college. Attractive riverside gardens with plant display, herbaceous and shrub borders; arboretum; a range of outdoor and protected commercial crops at Mansionfield Unit, together forming part of a horticultural teaching & research department. Additional features this year include Farm Walk and Vintage Vehicle Display. Car parking free. Afternoon Tea in Refectory.

Wide selection of pot plants, shrubs & Auchincruive honey for sale.

Ayr 3m. Route B743.

Admission £3.00 Children under 14 free OAPs £1.50

SUNDAY 18th MAY 1 - 5.30 pm

40% between Erskine Hospital, the Scottish War Blind and the British Red Cross Society

---

BARDROCHAT, Colmonell   ♿ (partly)
(Mr & Mrs Alexander McEwen)

Landscaped by Lorimer. Walled garden built by Lorimer but has been redesigned by present owners. Herbaceous, vegetables and potager. Conservatory. Spectacular views from the lawn. Garden as seen on 1994 'Beechgrove Garden'. Lawn and conservatory suitable for wheelchairs but please state at gate. Pipe band. Teas. Girvan 12 miles, Colmonell ½ mile - will be signposted.

Admission £1.50 Children 50p

SUNDAY 10th AUGUST 2 - 5.30pm

40% to Cancer Relief Macmillan Fund

BARGANY, Girvan   ♿
(N J F Dalrymple Hamilton)

This woodland garden has a lily pond with island, surrounded by masses of yellow, pink and white azaleas, and a huge variety of species rhododendron flowering from April to June. In conjunction with many fine hard and softwood trees, there is a small rock garden and spring displays of daffodils and snowdrops, and autumn colours. Plant stall. Route: take B734 from Girvan towards Dailly, four miles on left.

Admission: Contribution box

1st MARCH – 31st OCTOBER 10am–7pm or dusk

Donation to Scotland's Gardens Scheme

BARNWEIL, Craigie, near Kilmarnock   ♿
(Mr & Mrs Ronald Alexander)

A garden which has been developed from scratch during the last 20 years. Formally planned and colour co-ordinated herbaceous and some shrub rose borders surround the house. These give way to the woodland garden which features rhododendrons, azaleas, ferns, meconopsis and primulas, as well as a golden border. Other features of the garden are beech, and mixed beech and holly hedges, which provide much needed shelter on this rather exposed site. On a clear day, there are fine views to the north for 60-70 miles to Ben Lomond and beyond. Home baked teas. Cars free. Craigie 2 miles. Route: right off B730, 2 miles south of A77.

Admission £1.50 Children under 12 free

SUNDAY 8th JUNE 2 - 5 pm

40% to Tarbolton Parish Church

BLAIR, Dalry
(Mrs M G Borwick)
The extensive and fine-timbered policies surrounding this tower house of great antiquity, are first mentioned by Pont in the early 17th century. The well laid out park is attributed to Captain William Fordyce Blair RN in the 1850s. Visitors are permitted to walk through these delightful historic grounds all the year round and will find much to admire and enjoy. Route: from A737 in Dalry go to railway station. Entrance $\frac{1}{2}$ mile beyond station.
OPEN ALL YEAR
Donations to Scotland's Gardens Scheme. Ask at house.

BLAIRQUHAN, Straiton, Maybole &
(Mr James Hunter Blair)
Castle in Tudor style designed by William Burn, 1820-24 for Sir David Hunter Blair, 3rd Bart. Sixty-foot high saloon with gallery. The kitchen courtyard is formed with stones and sculpture from an earlier castle. All the original furniture made for the house is still in it. There is a good collection of pictures and a gallery of paintings by the Scottish Colourists. Three mile private drive along the River Girvan. Walled garden with herbaceous border and Regency glasshouse. The Castle is surrounded by an extensive park including an arboretum. Admission price includes tour of house. Tea in house. One mile west of Straiton. Entry from B7045.
Admission £3.50   Children £2.00   OAPs £2.50
SUNDAY 17th AUGUST 1.30 - 4.30 pm
20% to Ayrshire Hospice   20% to Kyle & Carrick Civic Society

---

CARNELL, Hurlford &
(Mr & Mrs J R Findlay)
Alterations in 1843 by William Burn. 16th century peel tower. Walled garden, rock and water gardens; 100 yards herbaceous border and new 100 yard phlox and shrub border. Herbaceous borders around Carnell House with extensive Plant Sale. Home baking stall. Silver band. Ice cream and cream teas. Cars free. Kilmarnock 6 miles. Mauchline 4 miles on A76. $1\frac{1}{2}$ miles on Ayr side of A719.
Admission £2.00 School children free
SUNDAY 27th JULY 2 - 5.30pm
40% between Craigie Parish Church & Craigie Village Hall, Hansel Village, the British Red Cross Society and The Association for International Cancer Research

---

CULZEAN CASTLE & COUNTRY PARK, Maybole   &
(The National Trust for Scotland)
Former tower house, castellated and remodelled by Robert Adam 1777–92, complete with viaduct, stables and home farm. Three main garden areas, the Fountain Court (a terraced garden in front of the Castle with an Orangery), the Walled Garden and Herb Garden (herbaceous, semi-tropical trees, shrubs and plants) and Happy Valley (a wild woodland garden with specimen trees and shrubs). Visitor Centre & Restaurant, newly restored Camellia House (originally an orangery), deer park, woodland walks, ranger-led excursions, events programme, swan pond and other exhibitions. Route: A719, Maybole 4 miles. Combined ticket for Castle & Country Park: £6/£4. Family £16. Country Park only: £3/£2 Family £8.
Open 1 Apr or Good Friday if earlier - 31 Oct 10.30am-5pm.
SUNDAY 13th APRIL, SUNDAY 4th MAY & THURSDAY 10th JULY
Scotland's Garden Scheme Tour 2 - 3.30pm.
40% to The Gardens Fund of The National Trust for Scotland
For other opening details see page 125

FAIRLIE GARDENS

Fairdene, 9 Montgomerie Avenue. (Mr & Mrs J Wotherspoon)
Plantsman's garden specialising in alpine plants and sun lovers suitable for a mild coastal climate. Plant stall.
Fairlieburne Cottage, 13 Main Road. (Mr & Mrs A Jarvie)
Cottage garden with water features. Tea and biscuits. Plant stall.
Route: A78, signposted in village. Admission £1.50 Children 50p, includes both gardens
SATURDAY 14th JUNE 2 - 5pm
20% Crossroads Care Attendant Scheme 20% Fairlie Parish Church

KINGENCLEUCH HOUSE GARDEN, Mauchline &. (limited)

(Sir Claud & Lady Hagart-Alexander)
$3\frac{1}{2}$ acres of informal garden containing the Scottish Collection of Leucanthemum x superbum (Shasta daisy) and trillium, plus $1\frac{1}{2}$ acres of woodland/glen walk. Teas. Plant stall. One mile south of Mauchline on A76.
Admission £1.50 Children 75p
SUNDAY 13th JULY 2 - 5.30pm
40% to St Ninians Church, Prestwick (BIFF Fund)

MARTNAHAM LODGE, by Ayr &. (partly)

(Colonel Sir Bryce Knox)
Situated on the edge of Martnaham Loch with important habitat for birds. Shrubs. Woodland walk. Tea and biscuits in house. Route: On B742 between A713 and A70.
Admission £1.50 Children under 12 free
SUNDAY 15th JUNE 2 - 5pm
40% to British Red Cross (Ayrshire & Arran branch)

PENKILL CASTLE, near Girvan &. (limited)

(Mr & Mrs Patrick Dromgoole)
A series of three Victorian gardens, vegetable, formal and landscaped, linked by a "wild walk" overlooking a burn leading to the Penwhapple river. Currently undergoing restoration work by the present owners. Teas. Route: 3 miles east of Girvan on Old Dailly to Barr road.
Admission £1.60
SUNDAY 29th JUNE 2 - 5pm
40% to Barr Parish Church

SKELDON, Dalrymple

(Mr S E Brodie QC & Mrs Brodie)
One and a half acres of formal garden and four acres of woodland garden in unique setting on the banks of the River Doon. Large collection of rhododendrons and azaleas, substantial glasshouse collection. Home baked teas. Silver band on the lawn. Plants for sale. Cars free. Dalrymple, B7034 between Dalrymple and Hollybush.
Admission £2.00 Children & OAPs £1.00
SUNDAY 3rd AUGUST 2 - 6 pm
40% to the Mental Health Foundation

BERWICKSHIRE

District Organiser:	**Col S J Furness,** The Garden House, Netherbyres, Eyemouth TD14 5SE
Area Organisers:	**The Hon Mrs Charles Ramsay,** Bughtrig, Leitholm, Coldstream TD14 4JP
	Miss Jean Thomson, Stable Cottage, Lambden, Greenlaw, Duns TD10 6UN
Hon. Treasurer:	**Mr Richard Melvin,** Bank of Scotland, 88 High Street, Coldstream TD12 4AQ

DATES OF OPENING

Bughtrig, Leitholm .... June– September 11am – 5pm, or by appointment
The Hirsel, Coldstream .... Open daily all year, reasonable daylight hours
Manderston, Duns .... Sundays & Thursdays 18 May – 28 September

Netherbyres, Eyemouth .... Sunday 20 April	2 - 6pm
Charterhall, Duns .... Sunday 25 May	2 - 5pm
Manderston, Duns .... Monday 26 May	2-5.30pm
Whitchester House, Duns .... Sunday 1 June	2 - 5.30pm
Bughtrig, Leitholm .... Sunday 29 June	2.30-5pm
Shannobank, Abbey St Bathans .... Sunday 13 July	2 - 5pm
Netherbyres, Eyemouth .... Sunday 20 July	2 - 6pm
Manderston, Duns .... Monday 25 August	2-5.30pm

BUGHTRIG, Near Leitholm, Coldstream ⅚ (mainly)
(Major General & The Hon Mrs Charles Ramsay)
This is a traditional Scottish family garden, hedged rather than walled and close to the house. It is an interesting combination of herbaceous plants, shrubs, annuals, vegetables and fruit. it is surrounded by fine specimen trees which provide remarkable shelter. Small picnic area. Parking. Special arrangements are Half mile east of Leitholm on B6461.
Admission £1.50 OAPs £1.00 Children under 18 50p
SUNDAY 29th JUNE 2.30 - 5pm. Stalls.
40% to Christ Church, Duns
Open daily JUNE to SEPTEMBER 11am-5pm or by appt: 01890 840678
Donation to Scotland's Gardens Scheme

CHARTERHALL, Duns ♿

(Mr & Mrs Alexander Trotter)

Hybrid rhododendrons and azaleas in mature grounds. Flower garden, surrounding modern house. Small greenhouse and vegetable garden. Tea with home bakes and biscuits. Plant stall. 6 miles south west of Duns and 3 miles east of Greenlaw on B6460.
Admission £1.50   Children 50p

SUNDAY 25th MAY 2 - 5 pm

40% to Scottish Dyslexia Trust

THE HIRSEL, Coldstream ♿ (mainly)

(The Earl of Home CBE)

Snowdrops and aconites in Spring; daffodils in March/April; rhododendrons and azaleas in late May/early June, and magnificent autumn colouring. Walks round the lake, Dundock Wood and Leet valley. Marvellous old trees. Dogs on leads, please. Homestead Museum, Craft Centre and Workshops. Tearoom (parties please book). Immediately west of Coldstream on A697. Parking charge only.

OPEN DAILY ALL YEAR (Reasonable daylight hours)

Donation to Scotland's Gardens Scheme

MANDERSTON, Duns ♿

(The Lord Palmer)

The swan song of the great classical house. Formal and woodland gardens. Tearoom in grounds. 2 miles east of Duns on A6105. Buses from Galashiels and Berwick. Alight at entrance on A6105.
Admission: Prices unavailable at time of going to press.

SUNDAYS & THURSDAYS 18th MAY to 28th SEPTEMBER,
HOLIDAY MONDAYS 26th MAY and 25th AUGUST 2 - 5.30 pm

Parties any time by appointment. Tel: 01361 883450

Donation to Scotland's Gardens Scheme

NETHERBYRES, Eyemouth ♿

(Col S J Furness & GRBS)

Unique 18th century elliptical walled garden, with a new house built inside. Daffodils and wild flowers in the spring. Annuals, roses, herbaceous borders and coloured borders during the summer. Produce stall. Teas in house. Eyemouth ¼ mile on A1107.
Admission £1.50   Children 50p

SUNDAY 20th APRIL 2 - 6 pm

40% to Eyemouth Museum Trust

SUNDAY 20th JULY 2 - 6 pm

40% to St Ebba's Church

SHANNOBANK, Abbey St Bathans

(Mr John Dobie)

A new garden created in the last 10 years on an exposed site surrounding a farmhouse and outbuildings with superb views. A mixture of fruit, ornamental trees, shrub roses, hardy shrubs and perennials. Woodland walks. Teas available at Riverside Restaurant, Abbey St Bathans. Half mile north west of Abbey St Bathans between Duns (7m) and Grantshouse signposted on A6112 and B6355.
Admission £1.50

SUNDAY 13th JULY 2 - 5pm

40% to Abbey St Bathans Village Hall Fund

WHITCHESTER HOUSE, Duns ♿
(Kings Bible College)
Rhododendrons and azaleas. Walled garden. A once famous garden which the owners are trying hard to restore with their own labour. Teas. Duns 7 miles, off B6355.
Admission £1.50 Children free
SUNDAY 1st JUNE 2 - 5.30pm
40% to Kings Bible College

CAITHNESS & SUTHERLAND

Joint District Organisers:	**Mrs Robert Howden,** The Firs, Langwell, Berriedale, Caithness KW7 6HD
	Mrs Colin Farley-Sutton, Shepherd's Cottage, Watten, Caithness KW1 5YJ
Area Organiser:	**Mrs Richard Tyser,** Gordonbush, Brora KW9 6LX
Hon. Treasurer:	**The Manager,** Clydesdale Bank plc, 17 Trail Street, Thurso KW14 7EL

DATES OF OPENING

Dunrobin Castle, Golspie	Saturday 21 June	10.30am – 5.30pm
Castle of Mey	Wednesday 16 July	2 – 6pm
Castle of Mey	Thursday 24 July	2 – 6pm
House of Tongue, Tongue	Saturday 2 August	2 – 6pm
Sandside House, Reay	Sunday 3 August	2 - 5pm
Langwell, Berriedale	Sunday 10 August	2 – 6pm
Langwell, Berriedale	Sunday 17 August	2 – 6pm
Dunbeath Castle, Dunbeath	Sunday 24 August	2 - 6pm
Castle of Mey	Saturday 6 September	2 – 6pm

CASTLE OF MEY, Mey, Caithness ♿
(H.M. Queen Elizabeth The Queen Mother)
Z-plan castle formerly the seat of the Earls of Caithness. 18th and 19th century additions. Remodelled 1954. Old walled-in garden. On north coast and facing the Pentland Firth and Orkney. Cars free. Teas served under cover. Mey 1½ mile. Route A836. Bus: Please enquire at local bus depots. Special buses can be arranged.
Admission £1.50 Children under 12 £1.00 OAPs £1.00
WEDNESDAY 16th JULY 2 - 6pm
40% to Scottish Disability Foundation (Edinburgh)
THURSDAY 24th JULY and SATURDAY 6th SEPTEMBER 2 - 6pm
40% to Queen's Nursing Institute (Scotland)

DUNBEATH CASTLE, Dunbeath   ♿
(Mr & Mrs Stanton Avery)

Traditional walled garden recently re-landscaped and containing magnificent display of herbaceous and greenhouse plants, together with vegetable garden and heather corner. Short woodland walk. Teas served in former coach house. Route: A9 to Dunbeath village Post Office, then follow old A9 south for 1¼ miles to castle gates.

Admission £1.50 Children under 12 and OAPs £1.00

SUNDAY 24th AUGUST 2 - 6pm

40% to Cancer Relief Macmillan Fund

DUNROBIN CASTLE & GARDENS, Golspie
(The Sutherland Trust)

Formal gardens laid out in 1850 by the architect, Barry. Set beneath the fairytale castle of Dunrobin. Tearoom and gift shop in castle. Picnic site and woodland walks. Dunrobin Castle Museum in the gardens. Suitable for disabled by prior arrangement. Group admission: Adults £4.40, children & OAPs £2.80, family £14.00. Castle one mile north of Golspie on A9.

Admission £4.80 Children & OAPs £3.20

SATURDAY 21st JUNE 10.30 am - 5.30 pm. (Last admission 5 pm)

40% to the British Lung Foundation

HOUSE OF TONGUE, Tongue, Lairg ♿ (partially)
(The Countess of Sutherland)

17th century house on Kyle of Tongue. Walled garden, herbaceous borders, old fasioned roses. Teas available at the Ben Loyal and Tongue Hotels. Tongue half a mile. House just off main road approaching causeway.

Admission to garden £1.50 Children 50p

SATURDAY 2nd AUGUST 2 - 6 pm

40% to the Royal Scottish Society for the Prevention of Cruelty to Children

---

LANGWELL, Berriedale ♿
(The Lady Anne Bentinck)

A beautiful old walled-in garden situated in the secluded Langwell strath. Charming access drive with a chance to see deer. Cars free. Teas served under cover. Berriedale 2 miles. Route A9.

Admission £1.50 Children under 12 & OAPs £1.00

SUNDAY 10th AUGUST and SUNDAY 17th AUGUST 2 - 6 pm

40% to Royal National Lifeboat Institution

SANDSIDE HOUSE GARDENS by Reay, Thurso ♿ (partially)
(Mr & Mrs Geoffrey Minter)

Old walled gardens being restored but well stocked. Sunken rectangular walled garden. Upper garden with sea views to the Orkneys and Grade A listed 2-seater privy. Terrace with rockery overlooking sunken garden. Main gate is on A836 half mile west of Reay village. Teas. There is a splayed entrance with railings and gate lodge.

Admission £1.50 Children under 12 £1.00

SUNDAY 3rd AUGUST 2 - 5pm

40% to The Highland Hospice

CENTRAL

District Organiser: **Lady Edmonstone,** Duntreath Castle, Blanefield G63 9AJ

Area Organisers: **Mrs John Carr,** Duchray Castle, Aberfoyle FK8 3XL

Mrs Guy Crawford, St Blanes House, Dunblane FK15 0ER

Mrs Robin Hunt, Keirhill, Balfron G83 0LG

Mrs John Stein, Southwood, Southfield Crescent, Stirling FK8 2QJ

Mrs Patrick Stirling-Aird, Old Kippenross, Dunblane FK15 0CQ

The Hon Mrs R E G Younger, Old Leckie, Gargunnock FK8 3BN

Hon. Treasurer: **Mr A Kingsley,** Royal Bank of Scotland, 82 Murray Place, Stirling FK8 2DR

DATES OF OPENING

Daldrishaig House, Aberfoyle .... May to July, by appointment
Kilbryde Castle, Dunblane .... All year, by appointment

Kilbryde Castle, Dunblane .... Sunday 16 March	2 – 4pm
Kilbryde Castle, Dunblane .... Sunday 13 April	2 – 5pm
Kilbryde Castle, Dunblane .... Sunday 4 May	2 – 5pm
The Pass House, Kilmahog .... Sunday 4 May	2 – 5.30pm
Touch, Cambusbarron .... Sunday 18 May	2 - 5pm
Kilbryde Castle, Dunblane .... Sunday 25 May	2 – 5pm
Arndean, by Dollar .... Sunday 1 June	2 - 6pm
Kilbryde Castle, Dunblane .... Sunday 8 June	2 – 5pm
Lochdochart, Crianlarich .... Sunday 8 June	12 - 5pm
Daldrishaig House, Aberfoyle .... Wednesday 11 June	2 – 5pm
The Walled Garden, E Lodge, Gean, Alloa .... Sunday 15 June	2 - 5pm
Callander Lodge, Callander .... Sunday 22 June	2 - 5pm
Kilbryde Castle, Dunblane .... Sunday 29 June	2 – 5pm
Orchardlea House, Callander .... Sunday 6 July	2 - 5pm
Kilbryde Castle, Dunblane .... Sunday 13 July	2 - 5pm
Burnbrae, Killearn .... Sunday 3 August	2 - 5pm
Kilbryde Castle, Dunblane .... Sunday 10 August	2 – 5pm
Thorntree, Arnprior .... Sunday 24 August	2 - 5pm
Kilbryde Castle, Dunblane .... Sunday 7 September	2 – 5pm
Kilbryde Castle, Dunblane .... Sunday 12 October	2 – 5pm

ARNDEAN, by Dollar
(Colonel & Mrs R Stewart)
Flowering shrubs, rhododendrons, azaleas. Woodland walk. Tea in stable yard and cottage. Route: off A977.
Admission £1.00 Children & OAPs 50p
SUNDAY 1st JUNE 2 - 6pm
40% to Strathcarron Hospice

BURNBRAE, Kirkhouse Road, Killearn
(Mr & Mrs C Russell Bruce)
Beautifully kept large Scottish country garden. Teas. At Glasgow end of Killearn village which is signposted off A81, 3 miles north of Strathblane.
Admission £1.00 Children free
SUNDAY 3rd AUGUST 2 - 5pm
40% to Scottish Bach Consort

CALLANDER LODGE, Leny Feus, Callander
(Miss Caroline Penney)
Romantic Victorian garden. Three acres of mature trees, specimen shrubs, lawns and herbaceous borders. Waterfall pool and fern grotto. Bog garden. Harmony walk. Tea & biscuits. Plant stall. Route: A84 west through Callander, turn right at sign to Leny Feus. Garden is at end on left.
Admission £1.50
SUNDAY 22nd JUNE 2 - 5pm
40% to Camphill Blair Drummond

DALDRISHAIG HOUSE, Aberfoyle
(Mr & Mrs J Blanche)
2 ½ acre plantsman's garden created in the last eight years. Water, scree and herbaceous gardens with little surprises. Home made teas. Garden pottery and plant stalls. Continue straight through Aberfoyle towards Kinlochard for 1½ miles. Very restricted parking. Please use free minibus service from Aberfoyle car park. Small and large private parties welcome by appointment in May, June & July. Tel: 01877 382223.
Admission £1.50 Children free
WEDNESDAY 11th JUNE 2 - 5 pm
40% to Crossroads Care Attendant Scheme

KILBRYDE CASTLE, Dunblane, Perthshire ᕃ (partly)
(Sir Colin & Lady Campbell & Mr J Fletcher)
Traditional Scottish baronial house rebuilt 1877 to replace building dating from 1461. Partly mature gardens with additions and renovations since 1970. Lawns overlooking Ardoch Burn with wood and water garden still to be completed. Three miles from Dunblane and Doune, signposted from both. No teas. No dogs. Children to be controlled. No toilets. Plants usually for sale.
Admission £2.00 Children under 16 and OAPs £1.50
SUNDAYS 16th MARCH 2 - 4 pm, 13th APRIL, 4th & 25th MAY, 8th & 29th JUNE, 13th JULY, 10th AUGUST, 7th SEPTEMBER, 12th OCTOBER 2 - 5pm.
40% to Leighton Library, Strathcarron Hospice, Cancer Relief Macmillan Fund and the Friends of Dunblane Cathedral
Also by appointment. Tel: 01786 823104

LOCHDOCHART, Crianlarich &

(Shona & John Christie)

Small, well planted, working kitchen garden created in two years from set-aside land. Rhododendrons and picnic beach on shore of Loch Iubhair. Home made teas. Plant and produce stall. Canoe hire and instruction. Bring your own picnic lunch. No dogs please. Route: A85 Perth to Stirling road. 13 miles north of Lochearnhead. Stone pillars on right.

Admission £1.00 Children free

SUNDAY 8th JUNE 12 - 5pm

40% to Crianlarich Pre-school Group

ORCHARDLEA HOUSE., Callander &

(Mr & Mrs R B Gunkel)

"Secret" garden of about half an acre with a wide variety of trees, shrubs, flowers and vegetables. Plant stall. Teas on the terrace. Sorry no dogs. Disabled parking only. At east end of Callander main street (A84). 5 mins. walk from centre of village.

Admission £1.00 Children free

SUNDAY 6th JULY 2 - 5pm

40% to Chest, Heart & Stroke Scotland

THE PASS HOUSE, Kilmahog, Callander & (partly)

(Dr & Mrs D Carfrae)

Well planted medium sized garden with steep banks down to swift river. Camellias, rhododendrons, azaleas, alpines and shrubs. Propagating house. Teas. Plant stall. 2 miles from Callander on A84 to Lochearnhead.

Admission £1.00 Children free

SUNDAY 4th MAY 2 - 5.30 pm

40% to Crossroads Care Attendant Scheme

THORNTREE, Arnprior &

(Mark & Carol Seymour)

Courtyard with flower beds all around. Small cottage garden created four years ago. Fern garden and small woodland underplanted with shade loving plants. Working dried flower area will be in full production in August. Teas. Plant stall. No dogs please. Route: A811. In Arnprior take Fintry Road, Thorntree is second on right.

Admission £1.50 Children over 12 50p

SUNDAY 24th AUGUST 2 - 5pm

40% Fintry Driving Group RDA

TOUCH, Cambusbarron & (partly)

(Mr & Mrs Patrick Buchanan)

Exceptionally fine Georgian house (also open - admission: £1.00) with superb interior. Interesting old documents and plans. Walled garden with mixed herbaceous and shrub borders, dwarf rhododendrons, magnolias and many other interesting shrubs. Garden continually expanding. Easy woodland walk with specie rhododendrons. Small plant stall. Simple teas available.

Admission £2.00 Children free

SUNDAY 18th MAY 2 - 5pm

40% to The National Trust for Scotland

THE WALLED GARDEN, East Lodge, Gean House, Alloa ♿

(Mr & Mrs A Scott)

One acre Victorian walled garden with original espaliered walks and central arbour. Mixed herbaceous borders. Large greenhouses. Recreated as faithfully as possible over the last five years. Woodland walk with decorative implements. Teas.

Take Stirling /Tullibody road straight through Tullibody. Second entrance on right after Jaegar factory.

Admission £1.00

SUNDAY 15th JUNE 2 - 5pm

40% to Enable

CLYDESDALE

District Organiser:	**Mrs J S Mackenzie,** The Old Manse, Elsrickle, Lanarkshire ML12 6QZ
Area Organiser:	**Miss A V Mackenzie,** Kippit Farm, Dolphinton, West Linton EH46 7HH
Hon. Treasurer:	**Mr M J Prime,** Elmsleigh, Broughton Road, Biggar, ML12 6AM

DATES OF OPENING

Baitlaws, Lamington	July - August by appointment	
Biggar Park, Biggar	May - August by appointment	
Dippoolbank Cottage, Carnwath	Sunday 15 June	2 - 6pm
Lawhead Croft, Tarbrax	Sunday 15 June	2 – 6pm
Carmichael Mill, Hyndford Bridge	Sunday 6 July	2 – 5pm
Dippoolbank Cottage, Carnwath	Sunday 20 July	2 - 6pm
Lawhead Croft, Tarbrax	Sunday 20 July	2 – 6pm
Baitlaws, Lamington	Sunday 27 July	2 - 5pm
Culter Allers, Coulter	Sunday 17 August	2 – 6pm

BAITLAWS, Lamington, Biggar
(Mr & Mrs M Maxwell Stuart)
The garden has been developed over the past seventeen years with a particular emphasis on colour combinations of hardy shrubs and herbaceous plants, many unusual. Set at around 900 ft above sea level, there are magnificent views of the surrounding hills. Large and varied plant stall. Teas. Route: off A702 above Lamington village. Biggar 5 miles, Abington 5 miles, Lanark 10 miles.
Admission £1.50 Children over 12 25p
SUNDAY 27th JULY 2 - 5 pm
By appointment JULY – AUGUST Tel: 01899 850240
40% to Biggar Museum Trust

BIGGAR PARK, Biggar 🕭 (partially)
(Mr & Mrs David Barnes)
Ten acre garden, starred in the 1997 Good Gardens Guide, incorporating traditional walled garden with long stretches of herbaceous borders, shrubberies, fruit, vegetables and greenhouses. Lawns, walks, pools and many other interesting features. Rhododendrons, azaleas and blue poppies in May and June. Good collection of old fashioned and new specie roses in July. Plants for sale sometimes. Interesting young trees.
Admission £2.00 by telephone appointment: 01899 220185.
Groups welcome MAY – AUGUST
Donation to Scotland's Gardens Scheme

CARMICHAEL MILL, Hyndford Bridge, Lanark 🕭 (partially)
(Chris & Ken Fawell)
Maturing riverside garden surrounding the only remaining workable water grain mill on the River Clyde a few miles upstream of the New Lanark textile mills. Informal and wild gardens with riverside walks, shrubberies, fruit and vegetables. Over 200 different ornamental trees. Also to be seen in the grounds evidence of the use of water power to medieval times including grain mills, foundry, lint mill and threshing mill. Friends of the Lanark Museum available to explain. Plant stall. Teas.
Admission £1.50 Children over 12 50p OAPs £1.00
Conducted tour of grain mill £1.00 extra
SUNDAY 6th JULY 2 - 5pm
40% to The Royal Burgh of Lanark Museum Trust

CULTER ALLERS, Coulter 🕭 (partially)
(The McCosh Family)
Culter Allers, a late Victorian gothic house, maintained its traditional one acre walled kitchen garden which continues to provide vegetables, fruit and flowers for the family. Peas and sweet peas, potatoes and poppies, cabbages and cornflowers, are bordered by box hedges. Areas of the kitchen garden have been opened out into lawn, a formal rose garden around a well, a herb garden and herbaceous borders. The remainder of the grounds are open and include a woodland walk, an avenue of 125 year old lime trees leading to the village church and a croquet lawn. Weather permitting, some classic vehicles will be on view. Plant stall. Teas. In the village of Coulter, 3 miles south of Biggar on A702.
Admission £1.50 Children free
SUNDAY 17th AUGUST 2 - 6 pm
20% to Coulter Library Trust   20% to Cancer Relief Macmillan Fund

DIPPOOLBANK COTTAGE, Carnwath
(Mr Allan Brash & children)

Artist's intriguing cottage garden. Vegetables grown in small beds. Herbs, fruit, flowers. Garden now extended to include pond, with flowers, trees, etc. Route: off B7016, 2½m Carnwath, 3m Auchengray Church Hall. Well signed. JOINT OPENING WITH LAWHEAD CROFT, TARBRAX.

Admission £1.50 Children 20p

SUNDAYS 15th JUNE and 20th JULY 2 - 6pm

40% to Cancer Relief Macmillan Fund

LAWHEAD CROFT, Tarbrax &
(Sue & Hector Riddell)

Cottage, 945 ft above sea level in open Lanarkshire countryside; 1½ acres garden subdivided into enclosures. Some mature, some new with alpine, bonsai, herbaceous, fruit, vegetables and pools, full of surprises - we're plant enthusiasts. Plants for sale. Teas by Auchengray ladies in Auchengray Church Hall, 2½m towards Carnwath - well signed. No dogs please. Route: A70, 12m Balerno, 6m Carnwath and Forth. Signposted from Tarbrax turning. JOINT OPENING WITH DIPPOOLBANK COTTAGE, CARNWATH.

Admission £2.00 Children 20p

SUNDAYS 15th JUNE and 20th JULY 2 - 6 pm

40% to Auchengray & District Charitable Association

Good at photography?

Details of our photographic competition are opposite page 65

DUMFRIES

District Organiser:	**Mrs Alison Graham,** Peilton, Moniaive, Thornhill DG3 4HE
Area Organisers:	**Mr W Carson,** 53 Castledykes Road, Dumfries DG1 4SN
	Mrs M Johnson-Ferguson, Springkell, Eaglesfield DG11 3AL
	Mrs Allen Paterson, Grovehill, Thornhill DG3 4HD
Hon. Treasurer:	**Mrs Alison Graham**

DATES OF OPENING

Arbigland, Kirkbean ....Tuesdays to Sundays: May - September 2 – 6pm
Also Bank Holiday Mondays

Barjarg Tower, Auldgirth .... Sunday 20 April	2 - 5pm
The Crichton, Dumfries.. Sunday 18 May	2 – 5pm
Craigieburn Garden, Moffat .... Sunday 8 June	12.30 – 8pm
The Garth, Tynron... Sunday 29 June	2 - 5pm
Sanquhar House, Sanquhar .... Sunday 13 July	2 - 5pm
Cowhill Tower, Holywood .... Sunday 20 July	2 - 5pm
Barony College Walled Garden, Parkgate .... Sunday 27 July	1 - 5pm
Dabton, Thornhill .... Sunday 17 August	2 - 5pm
Craigieburn Garden, Moffat .... Sunday 31 August	12.30 – 8pm

ARBIGLAND, Kirkbean
(Captain & Mrs J B Blackett)
Woodland, formal and water gardens arranged round a secluded bay. The garden where Admiral John Paul Jones worked as a boy in the 18th century. Cars free. Picnic area by sandy beach. Dogs on lead, please. Home baked tea in rustic tea room. Signposted on A710 Solway Coast Road.
Admission £2.00 Children over 5 50p OAPs £1.50
TUESDAYS TO SUNDAYS: MAY - SEPTEMBER 2 - 6 pm.
ALSO BANK HOLIDAY MONDAYS. House open 23rd May - 1st June incl.
Donation to Scotland's Gardens Scheme and SSAFA

BARJARG TOWER, Auldgirth
(Mr & Mrs J A Donaldson)
16th century tower with later additions. Daffodils. Display of Highland Dancing. Teas under cover. Route: 4 miles north of Auldgirth on Auldgirth-Penpont Road. Car parking free.
Admission £1.50 Accompanied children 50p
SUNDAY 20th APRIL 2 - 5pm
40% to St John's Church, Dumfries

THE BARONY COLLEGE WALLED GARDEN, Parkgate ♿

(The Barony College)

Teaching walled garden including glass houses, polytunnels, ornamental gardens, vegetable and fruit gardens. Experts on hand to give advice on gardening problems. Teas and plant stall. Follow signposts on A701 from Dumfries; approximately 10 miles north of Dumfries at Parkgate.

Admission £1.50 Children 50p

SUNDAY 27th JULY 1 - 5pm

40% to Headway, Dumfries branch

COWHILL TOWER, Holywood

(Captain & Mrs A E Weatherall)

Splendid views from lawn down Nith Valley. Interesting walled garden. Topiary animals, birds and figures. Woodland walks. Produce stall. Tea under cover. Holywood 1½ miles, off A76, 5 miles north of Dumfries.

Admission £1.50

SUNDAY 20th JULY 2 - 5pm

20% to Carnsalloch Cheshire Home   20% to British Red Cross Society

---

CRAIGIEBURN GARDEN, Moffat

(Janet Wheatcroft)

A plantsman's garden specialising in plants of south east Asia. A spectacular gorge and sheltered woodland provide ideal conditions for the National Collection of Meconopsis. Also formal borders, roses, bog garden, peat beds and alpines. Specialist plant nursery. Plants for sale. Route: 2 miles east of Moffat on A708 Selkirk road round bad bends on left, not right.

Admission £1.50 Children free

SUNDAYS 8th JUNE & 31st AUGUST 12.30 - 8pm

40% to the Gurkha Welfare Trust

THE CRICHTON, Dumfries

(Crichton Development Company)

Beautiful and extensive grounds of approx. 80 acres landscaped with mature rhododendrons, azaleas and many specimen trees, including Davidia involucrata (handkerchief tree) and Liriodendron tulipifera (tulip tree). Large rock garden complete with waterfall, ornamental pond and bog garden. The Crichton Memorial Church, an imposing red sandstone building, celebrates its centenary this year and there are many other listed buildings, including Easterbrook Hall. Many events on the day. Teas at Easterbrook Hall. Route: B725, Dumfries 1 mile.

Admission £1.50 Accompanied children 50p Cars free

SUNDAY 18th MAY 2 - 5 pm

40% to Crichton Royal Amenity Fund

DABTON, Thornhill ♿

(The Earl & Countess of Dalkeith)

Late 18th century house built of pink stone. Extensive walled garden. Herbaceous border 95 yards long, roses, island beds of trees and shrubs, pond, woodland walk, vegetable garden, greenhouses. Tea in old stables. Entrance off A76 between Thornhill and Carronbridge.

Admission £1.50 Accompanied children 50p

SUNDAY 17th AUGUST 2 - 5pm

40% to Cancer Relief Macmillan Fund, Thornhill Committee

 # THE GARTH, Tynron
(Mimi Craig & Jock Harkness)
Old manse, established 1750 with additions. 2 acre garden, woodland, waterside and walled garden. The walled garden is being reconstructed and much heavy maintenance has been achieved throughout. Teas in Tynron Village Hall. Route: off A702 between Penpont and Moniaive.
Admission £1.50, includes nearby gardens
SUNDAY 29th JUNE 2 - 5pm
40% to Village Hall Fund

SANQUHAR HOUSE, Sanquhar &
(Catriona McLean)
Old manse walled garden. Mature trees and new borders including herb garden, clematis, old roses and unusual hardy perennials. Teas. Cake and plant stalls. Car parking free. On A76 three-quarters mile north of Sanquhar opposite Sanquhar Academy.
Admission £1.50 Children 50p
SUNDAY 13th JULY 2 - 5pm
40% to Arthritis Research

DUNBARTONSHIRE WEST

District Organiser: **Mrs W A C Reynolds,** North Stanley Lodge, Cove, Helensburgh G84 0NY

Area Organisers: **Mrs T C Duggan,** Kirkton Cottage, Darleith Road, Cardross G82 5EZ

     Mrs James Dykes, Dawn, 42 East Abercromby Street, Helensburgh G84 9JA

     Mrs R C Hughes, Brambletye, Argyll Road, Kilcreggan, G84 0JY

     Mrs J S Lang, Ardchapel, Shandon, Helensburgh G84 8NP

     Mrs H G Thomson, 47 Campbell St., Helensburgh G84 9QW

Hon. Treasurer: **Dr D P Braid,** 41 Charlotte Street, Helensburgh G84 7SE

DATES OF OPENING

Auchendarroch, Tarbet .... 1 April-30 June by appointment
Glenarn, Rhu .... Daily 21 March–21 July, sunrise to sunset

Glenarn, Rhu .... Sunday 4 May		2 – 5.30pm
Auchendarroch, Tarbet .... Sunday 18 May		2 - 5.30pm
Geilston House, Cardross .... Saturday 24 May		2 – 5.30pm
Ross Priory, Gartocharn .... Sunday 25 May		2 – 6pm
The Linn Garden, Cove .... Sunday 1 June		2 – 6pm
Wards, Gartocharn .... Sunday 8 June		2 - 6pm
Old Court, Rhu .... Sunday 15 June		2 - 5.30pm
Geilston House, Cardross .... Sunday 20 July		2 – 5.30pm
The Hill House Plant Sale, Helensburgh ...... Sunday 7 September		11am – 5pm

AUCHENDARROCH, Tarbet
(Mrs Hannah Stirling)
Five acre garden, superbly set on shores of Loch Lomond. Wild garden, woodland walk, wide range of heathers, flowering trees and shrubs including cherries, rhododendrons and azaleas. Regal pelargoniums particularly notable. Plant stall. Dogs on lead only. Immediately south of Tarbet on A82, lower entrance gate beside Tarbet Pier.
SUNDAY 18th MAY 2 - 5.30pm
Tea and shortbread. Admission £1.00 Children free
1st APRIL to 30th JUNE by appointment. Tel. 01301 702240
40% to Friends of Loch Lomond

GEILSTON HOUSE, Cardross &
(Miss M E Bell)
Walled garden. Glen with burn. Azaleas, rhododendrons and flowering shrubs. Wild hyacinths. Herbaceous border and roses. P lant stall on 24th May. Sorry no dogs. Cars free. Teas. Cardross 1 mile. Route A814.
Admission £1.50 Children under 12 free
SATURDAY 24th MAY 2 - 5.30 pm
SUNDAY 20th JULY 2 - 5.30pm
All takings to Scotland's Gardens Scheme

GLENARN, Rhu

(Mr & Mrs M Thornley & family)

Woodland garden with burn, daffodils, primulas and bluebells by season, amongst a notable collection of rhododendrons, species and hybrids, as well as magnolias, embothriums and many other fine trees and shrubs. Restoration work in progress at the old pond. Collecting box. Dogs on lead please. No cars up drive. A814 between Helensburgh and Garelochead. Regular bus service, stop at Rhu Marina, up Pier Road to Glenarn Road.

Minimum donation £1.50 Children 50p (Scotland's Gardens Scheme)

DAILY 21st MARCH to 21st JULY, sunrise - sunset.

Special Opening SUNDAY 4th MAY 2 - 5.30pm.

Home made teas and plant stall. Admission £1.50 Children 50p.

40% to Sight Savers (Royal Commonwealth Society for the Blind)

THE HILL HOUSE, Helensburgh ♿ (garden only)

(The National Trust for Scotland)

SCOTLAND'S GARDENS SCHEME PLANT SALE in garden. The Hill House overlooking the estuary of the River Clyde, is considered the finest example of the domestic architecture of Charles Rennie Mackintosh. The gardens are being restored to Walter W Blackie's design with features reflecting the work of Mackintosh.

Admission to Plant Sale free. Donations to SGS welcome

House open separately 1.30 - 5pm. Admission may be restricted.

SUNDAY 7th SEPTEMBER 11 am - 5 pm

40% to The Gardens Fund of the National Trust for Scotland

For other opening details see page 133

THE LINN GARDEN, Cove

(Mr James Taggart)

Extensive collections of trees, shrubs, bamboos and water plants surrounding a classical Victorian villa with fine views over the Firth of Clyde. The Linn nursery attached to the garden will be open as usual for the sale of plants. Teas. Dogs on leads welcome. Entrance 1,100 yards north of Cove village on Shore Road, B833. No parking on Avenue; please park on shore side of main road.

Admission £2.50 Children under 12 free OAPs concession

SUNDAY 1st JUNE 2 - 6 pm

40% to Shelter (Scotland)

OLD COURT, Artarman Road, Rhu

(Mr & Mrs George Jeffrey)

Herbaceous borders, roses, shrubs, water garden, primulas. Tea and shortbread. Plant stall. Sorry, no dogs. Route: Helensburgh 1½ miles on A814. Bus stop opposite Rhu Marina.

Admission £1.00 Children free

SUNDAY 15th JUNE 2 - 5.30pm

40% to Erskine Hospital

ROSS PRIORY Gartocharn &

(University of Strathclyde)

1812 Gothic addition by James Gillespie Graham to house of 1693 overlooking Loch Lomond. Rhododendrons, azaleas, selected shrubs and trees. Walled garden with glasshouses, alpine beds, pergola, ornamental plantings. Family burial ground. Nature and garden trails. Putting Green. Baking and plant stalls. Tea in house. House not open to view. Cars free. Gartocharn 1½ miles off A811. Bus: Balloch to Gartocharn leaves Balloch at 1 pm and 3 pm.

Admission £1.50 Children free

SUNDAY 25th MAY 2 - 6 pm

20% to Enable   20% to Scottish Down's Syndrome Association

WARDS, Gartocharn & (partially)

(Sir Raymond & Lady Johnstone)

Interesting informal garden with mixed borders and water plants alongside natural streams and ponds in a unique setting. Garden merges into Loch Lomond National Nature Reserve. Walks through wild garden and to River Endrick and loch. Bird watching hide. Teas on house terrace or under cover . Plant stall. Sorry no dogs because of birds.

Also open: WARDS COTTAGE (by kind permission of Lady Robert Crichton-Stuart) Interesting cottage garden. Entrance off A811, 2½ miles west of Drymen, 1 mile east of Gartocharn village.

Admission £2.00 Children free

SUNDAY 8th JUNE 2 - 6pm

40% to SSPCA Milton Animal Welfare Centre

ARDCHATTAN PRIORY, NORTH CONNEL, Argyll
(Mrs Sarah Troughton)
Daily from 1st April to 30th October, 9 a.m.–6 p.m.
Fête on Sunday 20th July

Photograph by Brian Chapple

GREENFIELD LODGE, LASSWADE, Midlothian
(Alan and Helen Dickinson)
Tuesday 25th March, 2–5 p.m.
1st Tuesday in every month March to September, 2–5 p.m.

Photograph by Brian Chapple

EDZELL MAINS FARM, EDZELL VILLAGE, Angus
(Some village gardens in Edzell)
Sunday 27th July, 1.30–5.30 p.m.

Photograph by Brian Chapple

STRATHMORE COTTAGE, DRUMELDRIE, By UPPER LARGO, Fife
(Barbara Whitelaw and Bill Duncan)
Saturday 14th June, 1–5 p.m.

Photograph by Brian Chapple

DRUIMAVUIC HOUSE, APPIN, Argyll
(Mr and Mrs Newman Burberry)
Daily from 13th April to 29th June, 10 a.m.–6 p.m.

Photograph by Brian Chapple

PITTENWEEM SMALL GARDENS, Fife
(The Gardeners of Pittenweem)
Saturday and Sunday 9th and 10th August, 2–5.30 p.m.

Photograph by Brian Chapple

PHOTOGRAPH COMPETITION 1997

in association with
PHILLIPS SCOTLAND

In 1997 Scotland's Gardens Scheme is holding a competition to find the best colour photograph taken in a garden which is opening under the Scheme in 1997.

Phillips Scotland, the international auctioneers and valuers, have asked Charles Verey to donate the Lygrove seat shown below. This will be presented to the winner at the Annual General Meeting of the Scheme in November. The winning photograph will also appear in the 1998 edition of 'Gardens of Scotland', and at an exhibition to be held in Phillips saleroom. The owner of the garden will receive a cash voucher to spend at a Phillips Auction of garden ornaments.

Photographs should be taken at any garden on the day when it is open under Scotland's Gardens Scheme, unless there is a notice at the point of entry stating that photography is forbidden. If you wish to arrange to visit any garden outwith the opening times this can only be done by contacting the head office of Scotland's Gardens Scheme, who will try to arrange an appointment for you with the garden owner.

You may enter a total of ten photographs in all by completing the entry form overleaf, and following the instructions given. Extra forms may be obtained from the head offices of either Scotland's Gardens Scheme or Phillips.

Scotland's Gardens Scheme thanks Charles Verey (Tel: 01285 740561) for his most generous donation.

PHILLIPS
207 BATH STREET
GLASGOW G2 4HD
TEL: 0141 221 8377

SCOTLAND'S GARDENS SCHEME
31 CASTLE TERRACE
EDINBURGH EH1 2EL
TEL: 0131 229 1870

ENTRY FORM

Name ....

Address ....

....

.... **Postcode**........................

Daytime Telephone no ....

Which garden, from those open under the Scheme in 1997, does your photograph show?

....

Colour prints (9"x6" or 6"x9") and negatives or 35 mm colour slides should be sent to Scotland's Gardens Scheme, 31 Castle Terrace, Edinburgh EH1 2EL. Scotland's Gardens Scheme reserves the right to publish any photographs without prior permission of copyright owner.

The photographs are non returnable.

Panel of Judges:-

MRS M MAXWELL STUART   Chairman, Scotland's Gardens Scheme
CHRISTOPHER WESTON   Chairman, Phillips Fine Art Auctioneers
SIDNEY J CLARKE   Principal Photographer,
                             The Royal Botanic Garden Edinburgh

The decision of the judges is final.

Selected entries will be included in the 1998 handbook of Scotland's Gardens Scheme and also at an Exhibition to be held in Phillips saleroom.

Final entries to be sent to Scotland's Gardens Scheme office by the end of September 1997.

EAST LOTHIAN

District Organiser: **Lady Malcolm,** Whiteholm, Gullane EH31 2BD

Area Organisers: **Mrs J Campbell Reid,** Kirklands, Gullane EH31 2AL

Lady Fraser, Shepherd House, Inveresk, Musselburgh EH21 7TH

Mrs C Gwyn, The Walled Garden, Tyninghame, Dunbar EH42 1XW

Mrs M Ward, Stobshiel House, Humbie EH36 5PA

Hon Treasurer: **Mr R McGee,** Royal Bank of Scotland, 32 Court Street, Haddington EH41 3NS

DATES OF OPENING

Winton House, Pencaitland	Sunday 20 April	2 – 6pm
Inveresk, near Musselburgh	Tuesday 22 April	2 - 5pm
Tyninghame, Dunbar	Sunday 11 May	2 – 6pm
Elvingston House, by Gladsmuir	Sunday 18 May	2 - 6pm
Inveresk, near Musselburgh	Tuesday 20 May	2 - 5pm
Clint, Dunbar	Sunday 1 June	2 - 6pm
Stobshiel, Humbie	Sunday 15 June	2 - 5pm
Inveresk, near Musselburgh	Tuesday 17 June	2 - 5pm
West Fenton, North Berwick	Sunday 22 June	2 - 6pm
Stevenson House, nr Haddington	Sunday 29 June	1 - 5pm
Greywalls Hotel, Gullane	Monday 30 June	2 – 5pm
Forbes Lodge, Gifford	Sunday 6 July	2 – 6pm
Greywalls Hotel, Gullane	Monday 7 July	2 – 5pm
Gullane Gardens	Saturday 12 July	2 - 7pm
Luffness, Aberlady	Sunday 13 July	2 – 6pm
Inveresk, near Musselburgh	Tuesday 15 July	2 - 5pm
Athelstaneford Village	Sunday 20 July	2 - 6pm
Woodside, Gladsmuir	Sunday 27 July	2 - 5pm
SGS Plant Sale, Oxenfoord Mains, Dalkeith	Sunday 12 October	10.30am - 3pm

ATHELSTANEFORD VILLAGE
Several gardens in village of great historic interest. The Saltire flies permanently outside the kirk to celebrate "miraculous" appearance in sky of St Andrew's Cross before 8th century battle in which Pict and Scot defeated Anglo-Saxon Athelstan. Refreshments in village hall.
Admission £1.50 Children 10p
SUNDAY 20th JULY 2 - 6pm
20% to Riding for the Disabled Association, Muirfield group   *20% to Village Hall Funds*

CLINT, Dunbar
(Mr & Mrs John W Blair)
Rhododendrons in woodland setting, herbaceous and water gardens. Ideal for children. Teas. Plant stall. East Linton 3 miles, Stenton ½ mile. Down A1 turn right after East Linton bypass. After 2 miles, turn right B6370 to Gifford, drive entrance on left, exit through fields. Car park free.
Admission £1.50 Children 50p
SUNDAY 1st JUNE 2 - 6pm
40% to Malcolm Sargent Cancer Fund for Children

ELVINGSTON HOUSE, by Gladsmuir &
(Dr David & Mrs Janice Simpson)
18th century garden of Jacobean-baronial mansion. A Caithness stone fountain on the south lawn has been added recently and is surrounded by, in season, daffodils, 5,000 tulips and 1,000 roses. "Tetyana's Walk" is planted with roses, rhododendrons and spring bulbs; there is also a Laburnum and Fuschia Walk. 18th century cylindrical doocot with over 700 nesting boxes of ashlar stone. Teas. Dogs on lead please.
Route: 1 mile east of Gladsmuir, off A199 (old A1).
Admission £1.50 Children 50p Family Ticket £3.50
SUNDAY 18th MAY 2 - 6pm
20% to Congenital Heart Disease Fund, Royal Hospital for Sick Children
20% to Chernobyl Relief Foundation in the UK

FORBES LODGE, Gifford
(Lady Maryoth Hay)
Water garden. Old fashioned shrub roses. Burn. Stalls. Rare plants. Tea. Admission £1.00
SUNDAY 6th JULY 2 - 6 pm
40% to Children's League of Pity

GREYWALLS HOTEL, Gullane
(Mr & Mrs Giles Weaver)
Six acres of formal garden attributed to Gertrude Jekyll complements the Edwardian house built by Sir Edwin Lutyens in 1901. Rose garden, herbaceous, shrub and annual borders. Exhibition of contemporary sculpture and modern ornament organised by The Scottish Gallery.
Admission £2.50 Accompanied children free
MONDAYS 30th JUNE & 7th JULY 2 - 5pm
40% to Edinburgh Green Belt Trust

GULLANE GARDENS & (some)
Gateside House (Frank and Moira Kirwan)   **Grunnadal** (Bunty Grandison)
Kilbruach (Bob and Kathleen McInnes)   **Aldersyde** (Elizabeth Neil)
Attractive adjacent working gardens ranging up to one acre in size, in the conservation area of a delightful coastal village. Each garden has a distinct character and individual style, some are mature, some evolving. Together they offer a variety of layouts and a wide selection of alpines, shrubs, herbaceous and kitchen garden features. Teas. Plant stall. All gardens are on Nisbet Road; enter Gullane on A198, follow sign for beach; Nisbet road is first turn on left.
Admission £2.00 Children 50p OAPs £1.00 Family ticket £4.50, includes all gardens.
SATURDAY 12th JULY 2 - 7pm
20% to Chest Heart & Stroke Scotland
20% to Mamie Martin Fund to support education for girls in Malawi

INVERESK, near Musselburgh

Shepherd House (Sir Charles & Lady Fraser)
Catherine Lodge (Mr Philip Mackenzie Ross)

Two walled gardens in the 18th century village of Inveresk. Catherine Lodge, the larger of the two, with drifts of snowdrops, daffodils and crocus in spring, followed by magnificent herbaceous and rose borders. Well maintained traditional large vegetable garden and greenhouses. Shepherd House - a well planned one acre plantsman's garden with many unusual features, formal rill, ponds and fountains, alpine wall, old fashioned rose border and bower, potager and parterre. Large collection of tulips. No teas or stalls. Shepherd House also open by appointment : 0131 665 2570. Admission £2.00 (includes both gardens). Accompanied children free
TUESDAYS 22nd APRIL, 20th MAY, 17th JUNE, 15th JULY 2 - 5pm
40% to Friends of the Royal Botanic Garden Edinburgh

LUFFNESS, Aberlady ⅗ (weather permitting)
(Luffness Limited)
16th century castle with earlier foundations. Fruit garden built by Napoleonic prisoners-of-war. Tea in house. Plant stall. Donations please.
SUNDAY 13th JULY 2 - 6 pm
40% to Scottish Society for the Prevention of Cruelty to Animals

STEVENSON HOUSE, near Haddington ⅗
(Mrs J C H Dunlop)
House garden includes wide lawns surrounded by large flowerbeds containing a mixture of herbaceous plants and shrubs, a rose garden, spring border and rock edge. Woods and dell containing many fine trees. Formal walled garden, many unusual plantings. Plant stall. Riverside walk. Stevenson House marked on A1 between Haddington & East Linton. Historic House signs on A1 and on road from Haddington. Admission to grounds, including parking £2.50 Children under 12 free
SUNDAY 29th JUNE 1 - 5 pm
20% to Malcolm Sargent Cancer Fund for Children   20% to Save the Children Fund

STOBSHIEL, Humbie
(Mr & Mrs Maxwell Ward)
Walled garden adjacent to the house, box-edged borders with herbaceous plants, old fashioned roses and shrubs. Rustic summerhouse. Glasshouse. Shrubbery. Woodland walks and recently established water garden. Teas. Plant stall. Route: B6368 Haddington/Humbie roadsign, Stobshiel 1 mile.
Admission £1.50 Children 50p Family ticket £3.50
SUNDAY 15th JUNE 2 - 5pm
40% to Childrens Hospice Association Scotland

TYNINGHAME, Dunbar &

(Tyninghame Gardens Ltd)

Splendid 17th century pink sandstone Scottish baronial house, remodelled in 1829 by William Burn, rises out of a sea of plants. Herbaceous border, formal rose garden, Lady Haddington's secret garden with old fashioned roses, formal walled garden with sculpture and yew hedges. The 'wilderness' spring garden with magnificent rhododendrons, azaleas, flowering trees and bulbs. Grounds include one mile beech avenue to sea, famous 'apple walk', Romanesque ruin of St Baldred's Church, views across parkland to Tyne estuary and Lammermuir Hills. Tyninghame 1 mile.
Admission £1.50 Children 75p
SUNDAY 11th MAY 2 - 6 pm
40% to East Linton Support Group for St Columba's and Marie Curie Hospice

WEST FENTON, North Berwick

(Mr & Mrs W G Morrison)

Farmhouse garden redesigned over the last twenty years, with emphasis on colour combinations of hardy shrubs and herbaceous plants, many unusual. Several cottage gardens, planted in a variety of styles, may be visited at the same time. Teas. One mile south of Gullane. On A198 driving east, turn right just past Fire Training School. Farm is one mile along this road - red chimney landmark.
Admission £2.00 Accompanied children free
SUNDAY 22nd JUNE 2 - 6pm
40% to Riding for the Disabled Association (Muirfield group)

WINTON HOUSE, Pencaitland

(Sir David Ogilvy's 1968 Trust)

17th century Renaissance house. Decorative stone chimneys and dormers. William Wallace, master mason. Early 19th century castellated entrance. Beautiful plaster ceilings and stone carving, fine pictures and furniture. Masses of daffodils. Fine trees, terraced gardens. House conducted tour: £3.50, children under 14 £1.00. Tea and biscuits in house. From Pencaitland, lodge and wrought-iron gates two thirds of a mile on A6093, or, on B6355, archway and wrought-iron gates one mile from New Winton village, drive half a mile.
Admission £1.00 Children 25p
SUNDAY 20th APRIL 2 - 6 pm
40% to Royal Commonwealth Society for the Blind

WOODSIDE, Gladsmuir

The gardens of Woodside consist of Woodside House, Woodside Lodge, The Hayloft and The Granary, The Stables and North Woodside. Collectively they give a wide variety of garden styles and sizes, from the cottage garden to the country house garden, and include a woodside walk. Children's play area, tennis and croquet. Teas. Plant stall. Route: entrance off A199 (old A1) at Gladsmuir village and signed Woodside.
Admission £2.00 Children under 5 free OAPs £1.00 Family ticket £5.00
SUNDAY 27th JULY 2 - 5pm
40% to Save the Children Fund (still working in Scotland)

SGS PLANT SALE

A Bring and Buy Plant Sale will be held at Oxenfoord Mains, Dalkeith on
SUNDAY 12th OCTOBER 10.30am - 3pm.
Route: 4 miles south of Dalkeith on A68, turn left for one mile on A6093.
Admission free.

EDINBURGH & WEST LOTHIAN

Joint District Organisers: **Mrs J C Monteith,** 7 West Stanhope Place, Edinburgh EH12 5HQ

Mrs Charles Welwood, Kirknewton House, Kirknewton, West Lothian EH27 8DA

Joint Hon. Treasurers: **Mrs J C Monteith and Mrs Charles Welwood**

DATES OF OPENING

Newliston, Kirkliston	Wednesdays to Sundays inclusive 1 May – 4 June	2 – 6pm
Dalmeny Park, South Queensferry	Date to be announced	
Dean Gardens & Ann Street, Edinburgh	Sunday 13 April	2 – 6pm
Foxhall, Kirkliston	Sunday 20 April	2 – 5.30pm
Redhall Walled Garden, Edinburgh	Saturday 3 May	10am-3pm
Dr Neil's Garden, Duddingston	Sat & Sun 3/4 May	2 – 5pm
Regent Gardens, Edinburgh	Monday 19 May	2 – 5pm
Trefoil House, Gogarbank	Saturday 24 May	2 – 5pm
Grange, Linlithgow	Sunday 25 May	2 - 6pm
Redhall Walled Garden, Edinburgh	Saturday 31 May	10am-3pm
Moidart House, Currie	Sunday 8 June	1.30 - 4.30pm
Kirknewton House, Kirknewton	Sunday 15 June	2-6pm
Arthur Lodge, Dalkeith Road, Edinburgh	Sat & Sun 21/22 June	2 – 5pm
Malleny House Garden, Balerno	Wednesday 25 June	2 – 5pm
Suntrap Horticultural Centre, Edinburgh	Sunday 3 August	2 – 5pm
Dr Neil's Garden, Duddingston	Sat & Sun 9/10 August	2 – 5pm
Redhall Walled Garden, Edinburgh	Saturday 23 August	10am-3pm
SGS Plant Sale, Kirknewton House	Sat&Sun 27/28 September	11.30 - 4pm

ARTHUR LODGE, 60 Dalkeith Road, Edinburgh &
(Mr S R Friden)
Formal herbaceous garden. Sunken Italian garden and White garden. Plant stall. Teas.
Entrance to garden in Blacket Place, opposite the Commonwealth Pool.
Admission £1.50 Children £1.00
SATURDAY & SUNDAY 21st & 22nd JUNE 2 - 5pm
40% to Cockburn Association (Pinkerton Fund)

DALMENY PARK, South Queensferry

(The Earl & Countess of Rosebery)
Acres of snowdrops on Mons Hill. Cars free. Teas will be available in the Courtyard
Tearoom, Dalmeny House. Route: South Queensferry, off A90 road to B924.
Pedestrians and cars enter by Leuchold Gate and exit by Chapel Gate.
Admission £2.00 Children under 14 free
DATE TO BE ANNOUNCED
40% to St Columba's Hospice

DEAN GARDENS & ANN STREET, Edinburgh

DEAN GARDENS (Dean Gardens Committee of Management)
Privately owned town gardens on north bank of the Water of Leith. 13½ acres of
spring bulbs, daffodils, trees and shrubs and other interesting features. Entrance at Ann
Street or Eton Terrace.
ANN STREET GARDENS
Ann Street is one of the few Georgian streets where the houses on both sides boast their
own front gardens. They are particularly pretty in spring and early summer with
flowering trees, shrubs and bulbs.
Admission to both gardens £1.00 Children 50p
SUNDAY 13th APRIL 2 - 6 pm
All takings to Scotland's Gardens Scheme

DR NEIL'S GARDEN, Duddingston Village

(Drs Andrew & Nancy Neil)
Landscaped garden on the lower slopes of Arthur's Seat using conifers, heathers and
alpines. Teas in Kirk Hall. Plant stalls. Car park on Duddingston Road West.
Admission £1.25 Children free
SATURDAY & SUNDAY 3rd & 4th MAY 2 - 5 pm
SATURDAY & SUNDAY 9th & 10th AUGUST 2 - 5 pm
All takings to Scotland's Gardens Scheme

FOXHALL, Kirkliston

(Mr & Mrs James Gammell)
Daffodils and woodland walk. Plant stall. Cake stall.
Turn east at lights in centre of Kirkliston, half mile on
right, sign at road end, Conifox Nursery.
Admission £2.00 Children under 14 free OAPs £1.00
SUNDAY 20th APRIL 2 - 5.30 pm
40% to St Columba's Hospice

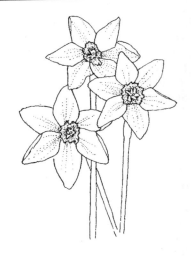

GRANGE, Linlithgow
(Mr & Mrs W A Cadell)
1909 Scottish baronial house on hillside overlooking Linlithgow Palace and loch. Azaleas, rhododendrons. Terraced garden with gazebos, rockery, woodland walk. Extensive views from garden and nearby Hope Monument on Airngath Hill. Exhibition of architectural drawings. Plant stall. Refreshments. Car parking free. Route: Linlithgow 2 miles. Bo'ness 2 miles. Off A706.
Admission £1.50 Children 75p OAPs £1.00
SUNDAY 25th MAY 2 - 6pm
40% to SSAFA

KIRKNEWTON HOUSE, Kirknewton &
(Mr & Mrs Charles Welwood)
Extensive woodland garden. Rhododendrons, azaleas and shrubs. Teas, weather permitting. No dogs please. Route: Either A71 or A70 on to B7031.
Admission £2.00 Children under 14 free
SUNDAY 15th JUNE 2 - 6pm
40% to St Columba's Hospice

KIRKNEWTON HOUSE, Kirknewton &
SGS Bring & Buy PLANT SALE
SATURDAY & SUNDAY 27th & 28th SEPTEMBER 11.30am - 4pm
40% to Childrens Hospice Association Scotland

MALLENY HOUSE GARDEN, Balerno &
(The National Trust for Scotland)
A two acre walled garden with 17th century clipped yew trees, lawns and borders. Wide and varied selection of herbaceous plants and shrubs. Shrub roses including NCCPG. 19th century rose collection. Ornamental vegetable and herb garden. Greenhouse display. Scottish National Bonsai Collection. Plant stall. Tea and biscuits. In Balerno, off Lanark Road West (A70) 7m from Edinburgh city centre. Buses: Lothian 43, Eastern Scottish, 66 & 44.
Admission £1.00 Children & OAPs 50p
WEDNESDAY 25th JUNE 2 - 5 pm
40% to The Gardens Fund of The National Trust for Scotland
For other opening details see page 133

MOIDART HOUSE, Blinkbonny Road, Currie &
(David & Jean Roberts)
Mature, three acre walled garden dating from 1850. Brae Burn runs through glen. Trees, shrubs, azaleas, rhododendrons, herbaceous garden in high yew hedges, box hedge borders, vegetable garden, greenhouses. Teas. Stall for produce. Route: A70 from Edinburgh. Left down hill, past Currie Kirk, up Kirkbrae. Turn first left, Moidart House on left before the corner and village of Blinkbonny.
Admission £2.00 Children under 14 free.
SUNDAY 8th JUNE 1.30 - 4.30pm
40% to Childline Scotland

NEWLISTON, Kirkliston &
(Mr & Mrs R C Maclachlan)
18th century designed landscape. Rhododendrons and azaleas. The house, which was designed by Robert Adam, is open and a collection of costumes will be on display. Teas. On Sundays tea is in the Edinburgh Cookery School which operates in the William Adam Coach House. Also on Sundays there is a ride-on steam model railway from 2 - 5 pm. Four miles from Forth Road Bridge, entrance off B800.
Admission to House & Garden £1 Children & OAPs 50p
WEDNESDAYS - SUNDAYS inclusive each week from1st MAY to 4th JUNE 2 - 6pm
40% to Childrens Hospice Association Scotland

REDHALL WALLED GARDEN, 97 Lanark Road, Edinburgh &
(Scottish Association for Mental Health)
A traditional walled garden built in the 18th century. Now a listed garden it is run on organic principles as a mental health project. Teas. Barbeque. Large selection of annuals, shrubs and herbaceous plants.
Admission 50p Children free
SATURDAYS 3rd & 31st MAY and 23rd AUGUST 10am - 3pm
40% to Scottish Association for Mental Health

REGENT GARDENS, Edinburgh
(Regent, Royal & Carlton Terrace Gardens Association)
Largest of the New Town gardens still in private ownership. Informally laid out in 1830 with lawns and wooded areas. Fine views over the Firth of Forth and towards Arthur's Seat. Plant stalls. Entrance at Carlton Terrace Lane.
Admission £2.00 Children £1.00
MONDAY 19th MAY 2 - 5pm
40% to Marie Curie Cancer Care

SUNTRAP HORTICULTURAL & GARDENING CENTRE, Gogarbank,Edinburgh &
(Oatridge Agricultural College, organised by Friends of Suntrap)
A horticultural out-centre of Oatridge Agricultural College. Compact garden of 1.7 hectares (3 acres), includes rock and water features, sunken garden, raised beds, woodland plantings & greenhouses. Facilities for professional and amateur instruction, horticultural advice and a place to visit. Home baking. Plant sales. Gardening advice. Parking for disabled drivers inside main gate, other car parking opposite. Signposted 0.5m west of Gogar roundabout, off A8 and 0.25m west of Calder Junction (City bypass) off A71. Bus route: Lothian Transit 37. Open daily throughout the year 9am - 4.30 pm. Friends of Suntrap in garden at weekends April to September 2.30 - 4.30pm.
Admission £1.00 Children & OAPs 50p
SUNDAY 3rd AUGUST 12 - 5pm
40% to The National Trust for Scotland (Newhailes Appeal)

TREFOIL HOUSE, Gogarbank &
Woodland walk and attractive gardens all suitable and accessible for disabled people. Plant stall. Souvenir shop and children's play area. Afternoon teas will be available. Ratho 2 miles, Edinburgh 6 miles. Westbound from Gogar roundabout, first left, follow signs, past Gogarburn and half mile past Suntrap. Westbound from Calder roundabout follow A71, first right to Hermiston and follow signs.
Admission £1.50 Children and OAPs £1.00
SATURDAY 24th MAY 2 - 5pm
40% to Trefoil House, Holiday Centre for People with Disabilities

ETTRICK & LAUDERDALE

District Organiser: **Mrs Gavin Younger,** Chapel-on-Leader, Earlston TD4 6AW
Hon. Treasurer: **Mr L Haldane,** Royal Bank of Scotland, High St., Melrose TD6 9PF

DATES OF OPENING

Bemersyde, Melrose .... Sunday 20 April	2 – 6pm
Carolside, Earlston .... Sunday 13 July	2 - 6pm
Mellerstain, Gordon .... Sunday 13 July	12.30 – 6pm
Abbotsford, Melrose .... Sunday 3 August	2 – 5.30pm

ABBOTSFORD, Melrose ♿ (partly)
(Mrs P Maxwell-Scott, OBE)
House and garden built and laid out by Sir Walter Scott, who built the house 1812-1832
when he died. Herbaceous and annual borders. Teashop in grounds. Jedburgh Branch
Royal British Legion Pipe Band. Admission to house and garden: £3.40, children £1.70.
Bus party - adults £2.35, children £1.20. Melrose 2 miles, Galashiels 1½ miles.
Admission to garden only: £2.00
SUNDAY 3rd AUGUST 2 - 5.30 pm
40% to Childrens Hospice Association Scotland

BEMERSYDE, Melrose ♿
(The Earl Haig)
16th century peel tower reconstructed in the 17th century with added mansion house.
Garden laid out by Field Marshal Earl Haig. Views of Eildon Hills. Woodland walks.
Admission to garden only. St Boswells via Clintmains or Melrose via Leaderfoot Bridge.
Admission £1.65 Children under 10 free
SUNDAY 20th APRIL 2 - 6 pm
40% to Lady Haig's Poppy Factory

CAROLSIDE, Earlston ♿
(Mr & Mrs Anthony Foyle)
18th century house set in parkland. A very traditional elliptical walled garden with a
beautiful collection of old roses and herbaceous border. Herb garden, oval rose garden
and mixed borders. Teas. Turn off A68 at sign one mile north of Earlston, six miles
south of Lauder.
Admission £2.00 Children free
SUNDAY 13th JULY 2 - 6pm
40% to St Andrews Church, Kelso

MELLERSTAIN, Gordon ♿
(The Earl of Haddington)
Adam mansion with formal terrace and rose garden. Extensive grounds with lake and
many fine trees. Tearoom in grounds. House open 12.30 - 5 pm; last admission 4.30
pm. Admission to House and Garden: £4.00, OAPs £3.00, Children £1.50. Route:
Gordon, 3 miles on A6089 or at turn off A6105 from A68 at Earlston 6 miles, both
signposted Mellerstain House. Admission to garden only: £1.50
SUNDAY 13th JULY 12.30 - 6 pm
Donation to Scotland's Gardens Scheme

FIFE

District Organiser: **Mrs David L Skinner**, Lathrisk House, Freuchie KY15 7HX

Area Organisers: **Mrs James Barr,** Burnbank, Drumhead, Saline KY12 9LL
Mrs A B Cran, Karbet, Freuchie KY15 7EY
Mrs Christine Gordon, The Tannery, Kilconquhar,
Leven KY9 1LQ
Mrs Roderick F Jones, Nether Kinneddar, Saline KY12 9LJ
Lady Spencer Nairn, Barham, Bow of Fife KY15 5RG
Mrs N Stewart-Meiklejohn, 6 Howard Place,
St Andrews KY16 9HL

Hon. Treasurer: **Mrs C Erskine,** Cambo House, Kingsbarns KY16 8QD

DATES OF OPENING

Cambo House, Kingsbarns .... Daily all year 10am – 5pm

Cambo House, Kingsbarns	Sunday 2 March (provisionally)	2 – 5pm
Barham, Bow of Fife	Sunday 4 May	12 - 4pm
Cambo House, Kingsbarns	Sunday 18 May	2 – 5pm
Whitehill, Aberdour	Sunday 25 May	2 - 5.30pm
3 Gardens in St Andrews	Sunday 8 June	2 - 5pm
Strathmore Cottage, Drumeldrie	Saturday 14 June	1 - 5pm
Culross Palace Garden	Sunday 15 June	11am – 5pm
Parleyhill, Culross	Sunday 15 June	11am - 5pm
Balcaskie, Pittenweem	Sunday 22 June	2 – 6pm
Gilston, Largoward	Sunday 22 June	2 - 5pm
St Andrews Botanic Garden	Sunday 29 June	10am – 6pm
Hill of Tarvit, Cupar	Sunday 6 July	12.30 – 5pm
Cambo House, Kingsbarns	Sunday 13 July	11am - 6pm
Kellie Castle, Pittenweem	Sunday 13 July	11am – 5pm
Crail Gardens	Sat & Sun 19/20 July	2 – 5.30pm
Balcarres, Colinsburgh	Sunday 27 July	2 – 5pm
Saline Country Gardens	Sunday 27 July	2 - 6pm
Falkland Palace Garden	Sunday 3 August	1.30 – 5pm
Parleyhill, Culross	Sunday 3 August	11am - 5pm
Pittenweem Gardens	Sat & Sun 9/10 August	2 – 5.30pm
Saline Village Gardens	Sunday 24 August	2 - 6pm
The Murrel, Aberdour	Sat & Sun 13/14 September	11- 5pm
Hill of Tarvit Plant Sale	Saturday 4 October	10.30am – 4pm
	Sunday 5 October	2 – 5pm

3 GARDENS in ST ANDREWS
166 South Street (Mr Henry Turner)
A cottage garden formed from a long rig, beside West Port in the heart of St Andrews.
30 Hepburn Gardens (Mrs Avril Sloan) &
A small-scale attempt to make an oblong garden interesting and colourful throughout the year. Plant stall. Opposite Donaldson Gardens.
Littleridge, Hepburn Gardens (Miss Penelope Uprichard) &
A town garden of character, looking over the Lade Braes and fronted by a huge eucalyptus tree. Teas. Plant stall. Dogs on lead welcome. At fork of Hepburn Gardens and Buchanan Gardens.
Admission £2.00, includes all 3 gardens. Accompanied children free
SUNDAY 8th JUNE 2 - 5pm
40% to The Malcolm Sargent Cancer Fund for Children

BALCARRES, Colinsburgh &
(The Earl & Countess of Crawford & Balcarres)
19th century formal and woodland garden; wide variety of plants. Teas. Plant stall.
½ mile north of Colinsburgh off A921.
Admission £2.50 Accompanied children free
SUNDAY 27th JULY 2 - 5 pm
20% to Colinsburgh SWRI   20% to Kilrenny Doocot Appeal, East Neuk Preservation Society

---

BALCASKIE, Pittenweem & (top terrace only)
(Sir Ralph Anstruther of that Ilk Bt.)
There has been a house, originally fortified, at Balcaskie since the 13th century and a charter granted to Ivor Cook by King Alexander III in 1223 exists. In 1665 Sir William Bruce altered the tower house, laid out the terraces and made what he called " the first mansion house in Scotland". He lived there before building, and moving to, Kinross house. The Anstruther family acquired the property in 1698. Teas. Stalls. East Neuk Pipe Band. Route: A917, 2 miles from Anstruther. Enter by west Lodge gate.
Admission £2.00 Children free
SUNDAY 22nd JUNE 2 - 6 pm
40% to SSAFA

BARHAM, Bow of Fife &
(Sir Robert & Lady Spencer Nairn)
A garden full of character and friends. A small woodland garden in the making with rhododendrons, shrubs, spring bulbs and ferns. Also a garden with herbaceous borders and island beds with shrubs and spring bulbs and a vegetable garden. Plant stall. Hot soup and rolls. Route: A91, 4 miles west of Cupar. No dogs please.
Admission £1.50 Children under 12 free
SUNDAY 4th MAY 12 - 4pm
40% to Pain Association Scotland

CAMBO HOUSE, Kingsbarns &

(Mr & Mrs T P N Erskine)

An enchanting unusual Victorian walled garden designed around the Cambo burn which runs through the garden and is spanned by ornamental bridges and a greenhouse. The garden supplies the superb Victorian mansion house (not open) with flowers, fruit and vegetables. An ornamental potager is planned for 1997. Woodland walk along the burn leads to the beach. The season starts with acres of snowdrops and snowflakes. Massed daffodils and spring bulbs follow. Over 220 named roses and herbaceous borders in summer. September borders and colchicum meadow give autumn interest. Cars free. Dogs on lead please. Route: A917.

Admission £2.00 Children free

OPEN ALL YEAR ROUND 10 am - 5 pm

SNOWDROP DAY: Provisionally SUNDAY 2nd MARCH 2 - 5pm Plant stall. Teas.
40% to Romania Link

SPRING OPENING: SUNDAY 18th MAY 2 - 5 pm Plant Stall. Teas.
40% to British Diabetic Association

ROSE OPENING: SUNDAY 13th JULY 11 - 6pm Refreshments
40% to Rose 2000 Appeal, Royal National Rose Society

CRAIL: SMALL GARDENS IN THE BURGH

(The Gardeners of Crail)

A number of small gardens in varied styles: cottage, historic, plantsman's, bedding. Exhibition of paintings at Lobster Cottage, Shoregate. Approach Crail from either St Andrews or Anstruther, A917. Park in the Marketgate. Tickets and map available only from Mrs Auchinleck, 2 Castle Street, Crail.

Admission £2.00 Acccompanied Children free OAPs £1.00

SATURDAY & SUNDAY 19th and 20th JULY 2 - 5.30 pm
20% to Childrens Hospice Association Scotland   20% to Crail Preservation Society

---

CULROSS PALACE GARDEN, Culross

(The National Trust for Scotland)

Built between 1597 and 1611, the house was not a Royal Palace, but the home of Sir George Bruce, a rich merchant. It features painted ceilings and has recently been restored and furnished. A model 17th century garden was created at the same time as the house restoration, and reflects what a successful merchant of the period might have grown to support his household - vegetables, culinary and medicinal herbs, soft fruit and flowering meads. Terraced and on a steep slope, it is laid out mainly in raised beds. Sections are partitioned by willow hurdle fences, and the path surface is made up of crushed shells.

Admission to Palace, garden, Town House and Study £4.00, concessions £2.70

Admission to garden £1.00 Children & OAPs 50p

SUNDAY 15th JUNE 11am - 5pm
40% to The Gardens Fund of the National Trust for Scotland

For other opening details see page 126

FALKLAND PALACE GARDEN, Falkland &

(The National Trust for Scotland)
The Palace was the hunting seat of the Stewart monarchs during the 15th and 16th centuries. The present garden was laid out after the last war on the site of the original Royal Garden and contains a Royal Tennis Court built in 1539 by Percy Cane and in play today. Tearooms nearby in village. Free car park. Route: A912.
Admission to Palace and garden £4.50, concessions £3.00.
Admission to Garden £2.30 Children £1.50
SUNDAY 3rd AUGUST 1.30 - 5 pm
40% to The Gardens Fund of the National Trust for Scotland
For other opening details see page 126

GILSTON, Largoward

(Mr Edward Baxter)
Late 18th century house with informal and wild gardens, primulas, meconopsis, rhododendrons and azaleas. Herbaceous and shrub borders. Wildflower meadow and butterflies. National Trust for Scotland and plant stalls. Teas. 8 miles from St Andrews, 6 miles from Leven on A915.
Admission £2.00 Accompanied children free
SUNDAY 22nd JUNE 2 - 5pm
40% to Largoward Parish Church

HILL OF TARVIT, Cupar

(The National Trust for Scotland)
Charming Edwardian mansion house designed in 1906 by Sir Robert Lorimer for jute magnate, Mr F B Sharp. Contains his fine collection of furniture, paintings, tapestries and Chinese porcelain. The house stands in beautiful grounds with many interesting and unusual plants, shrubs and trees. Heathers and heaths, rose garden and delightful woodland walk to toposcope. Perfect place for a picnic. Tea room. Plant stall.
Route A916. Admission to house and garden: £3.50, concesssions £2.30
Admission to garden: £1.00 Children & OAPs 50p
SUNDAY 6th JULY 12.30 - 5 pm
40% to The Gardens Fund of The National Trust for Scotland
For other opening details see page 127

**SCOTLAND'S GARDENS SCHEME
ANNUAL PLANT SALE, Hill of Tarvit**
Bring plants, buy plants. Large variety of shrubs and big clumps of herbaceous plants at bargain prices.
Saturday - Coffee & snack lunches. Sunday - Teas.
SATURDAY 4th OCTOBER 10.30am- 4pm
SUNDAY 5th OCTOBER 2 - 5pm
40% to East Fife Members Centre
of The National Trust for Scotland

KELLIE CASTLE, Pittenweem &

(The National Trust for Scotland)
A fine example of the domestic architecture of lowland Scotland. Lorimer exhibition and children's nursery. Walled organic garden features box edged paths, rose arches, herbaceous plants and shrub roses. Castle open 1.30-5.30pm, last entry 4.45pm. Admission to Castle and garden £3.50, concessions £2.30. Tearoom within castle available to those visiting garden only. Adventure playground. Good picnic area. Admission to Garden £1.00 Children & OAPs 50p
SUNDAY 13th JULY 11 am - 5 pm
40% to The Gardens Fund of the National Trust for Scotland
For further opening details see page 129

THE MURREL, Aberdour

(Mrs John E Milne)
This garden, which was planted in 1992 and is now reaching maturity, is worth a visit throughout the season as there is always something new to see. Features: shrubs, rhododendrons, roses (including shrub roses), rockeries, walled garden and woodland walks. Tea and biscuits. Plant stall selling only plants seen growing in garden. House not open. Garden not suitable for wheelchairs. No dogs please. On B9157 Inverkeithing/Kirkcaldy road, opposite Croftgarry Farm.
Admission £2.00
SATURDAY and SUNDAY 13th & 14th SEPTEMBER 11am - 5pm
All takings to Scotland's Gardens Scheme

PARLEYHILL GARDEN, Culross

(Mr & Mrs R J McDonald)
Overlooking the Forth and the historic village of Culross this delightful hidden garden is bordered by high stone walls and lies beside Culross Abbey and the adjacent Culross Abbey ruins. Pass around the house via the upper 'cool' garden (established in the early '60s) with its mature trees and a variety of shaded beds to discover the lower walled garden (dating from 1988) and its views. Here, take the chance to have a seat and enjoy the wide variety of plants and colourful display in the herbaceous borders full of old fashioned favourites like phlox, crocosmia, irises, asters etc. Plant stall selling a selection of plants from the garden. No dogs please. Free parking in village.
Admission £1.50 Accompanied children free
SUNDAY 15th JUNE 11am - 5pm with Culross Palace Garden
SUNDAY 3rd AUGUST 11am - 5pm in conjunction with Culross Burgh Medieval Fair
40% to Culross and Torryburn Church

PITTENWEEM: SMALL GARDENS IN THE BURGH

(The Gardeners of Pittenweem)
A good number of small gardens in varied styles, hidden in the streets and wynds of this beautiful and rather secretive burgh. Two excellent tea rooms in High Street. Many exhibitions of contemporary art running concurrently with garden openings. Festival in village starts 2nd August (until 10th) with torchlight parade and fireworks in evening. Nice dogs welcome. Tickets and map available only from Mrs M G Williamson, Priorsgait, 15 Cove Wynd. Route: A917.
Admission £2.00 Accompanied children free OAPs £1.00
SATURDAY & SUNDAY 9th & 10th AUGUST 2 - 5.30 pm
40% between Metabolic Diseases in Children Fund and Pittenweem Festival

SALINE COUNTRY GARDENS

A small number of farm and country gardens. Cars will be needed as gardens will be 2 miles outside village. One garden owner is a Seed Guardian for Henry Doubleday Research Vegetables. Good plant stall. Teas. Saline is five miles north-west of Dunfermline. Route: Junction 4 M90 and then on to B194. Maps and tickets will be sold in car park in centre of village. Gardens will be signposted.

Admission £2.00, includes all gardens   Accompanied children free

SUNDAY 27th JULY 2 - 6pm

40% to Crossroads Care Attendant Scheme, Fife

SALINE VILLAGE GARDENS

A number of small gardens and one large garden. Model railway will be running through one of the gardens. Teas in Church Hall.   Plant stall. Saline is five miles north-west of Dunfermline. Route: Junction 4 M90 and then on to B194. Cars can be parked in centre of village near bus stop, where maps and tickets will be sold. Gardens will be signposted. No dogs please.

Admission £2.00, includes all gardens   Accompanied children free

SUNDAY 24th AUGUST 2 - 6 pm

40% to Childrens Hospice Association Scotland

ST ANDREWS BOTANIC GARDEN, Canongate, St Andrews &

(Fife Council)

Peat, rock and water gardens. Tree, shrub, bulb and herbaceous borders. Large range of plants. Plant stall. Route: A915. Well signposted in St Andrews.

Admission £1.50   Senior citizens and accompanied children 50p

SUNDAY 29th JUNE 10 am - 6 pm

40% to Friends of the Botanic Garden

STRATHMORE COTTAGE, Drumeldrie, by Upper Largo

(Barbara Whitelaw & Bill Duncan)

A wonderful surprise comprising a succession of interlinked small gardens, each one filled with a wide range of plants from various continents. Teas. Plant stall. No dogs please. Approximately one mile east of Upper Largo on A917. Parking on grassland opposite.

Admission £2.00 Accompanied children free

SATURDAY 14th JUNE 1 - 5pm

40% to Cancer Relief Macmillan Fund (Fife group)

WHITEHILL, Aberdour   &

(Mr & Mrs Gavin Reed)

Shrubs and specie rhododendrons, a fine collection of interesting trees and lochan. Teas. Good plant stall. Route: B9157.

Admission £2.00

SUNDAY 25th MAY 2 - 5.30pm

40% to The Royal Blind Asylum & School

GLASGOW & DISTRICT

District Organiser: **Mrs J Thomson,** Hexagon House, Bardowie Loch G62 6EY

Area Organisers: **Mrs C M T Donaldson,** 2 Edgehill Road, Bearsden G61 3AD

Mrs P Oldfield, Bystone Mews, East Kilbride Road, Clarkston G76 8RU

Hon. Treasurer: **Mr M Smith,** 60 Cleveden Drive, Kelvinside G12 0NX

DATES OF OPENING

Invermay, Cambuslang .... April - September by appointment

Greenbank House & Garden, Clarkston .... Sunday 6 April	11am – 5pm
60 Cleveden Drive, Kelvinside .... Sunday 11 May	2 – 5pm
Hexagon House, Bardowie .... Sunday 8 June	2 - 5pm
Kittoch Mill, Carmunnock .... Sunday 6 July	2 – 5pm
Greenbank House & Garden, Clarkston .... Sunday 13 July	11am – 5pm
Whitemoss House, East Kilbride .... Sunday 10 August	2 – 5pm
35 Montgomerie Street, Eaglesham .... Sunday 10 August	2 - 6pm
Glasgow Botanic Gardens .... Sunday 17 August	12-4.45pm
SGS Plant Sale,	
Kilmardinny House Arts Centre, Bearsden .... Saturday 13 September	11am - 4pm

35 MONTGOMERIE STREET, Eaglesham
(Mr & Mrs James Laird)
A colourful country garden featuring beds of annuals, shrubs and mature trees, pond, new water feature and two wells. End of garden leads to open moorland. Home baked teas in nearby church hall. Plant stall. On B674 through village from East Kilbride to Ayrshire coast.
Admission £1.00 Children over 12 50p
SUNDAY 10th AUGUST 2 - 6pm
40% to Cancer Relief Macmillan Fund

---

60 CLEVEDEN DRIVE, Kelvinside ♿ (partly)
(Matthew Smith)
A plant person's communal garden with a little of everything - alpines, herbaceous, heathers and conifers, herbs, wildflowers, vegetables and small wildlife ponds all in a compact garden shared by nine flats. Good plant stall, with many unusual. Off Great Western Road, approx. half mile from the Botanic Gardens. Numerous buses, e.g. 66.
Admission £1.00 Children over 12 50p
SUNDAY 11th MAY 2 - 5pm
40% to NCCPG (Strathclyde)

GLASGOW BOTANIC GARDENS
(Glasgow City Council)
Visit Scotland's largest collection of filmy ferns. See behind the scenes in the tropical propagation houses where Glasgow's only 'Peepul' tree is grown. Don't miss the famous collections of exotic orchids, ferns, and one of the world's largest begonia collections. Teas. Corner of Queen Margaret Drive & Great Western Road. Leave motorway at Junction 17, follow signs for A82 Dumbarton.
Admission: Suggested donation £1.00 Children 50p
SUNDAY 17th AUGUST 12 - 4.45pm
All takings to Scotland's Gardens Scheme

GREENBANK HOUSE & GARDEN, Clarkston &
(The National Trust for Scotland)
Visitors will receive a warm welcome at the hidden jewel. Two-and-a-half acres of walled garden and 13 acres of policies surround an elegant Georgian house. The attractive garden shows how wide a range of ornamental plants, annuals, perennials, shrubs and trees can be grown in the area and is especially relevant to owners of small gardens. Guided garden walk with the Gardening Instructor, Mr Jim May, at 2.30pm. Tours of Greenbank House between 2pm and 5pm. Raffle. Plant Stall. Teas by The Friends of Greenbank. Clarkston 1mile. Bus: Strathclyde no.44D to Mearnskirk or Newton Mearns; alight at Flenders Road.
Admission to Garden £2.80 Children & OAPs £1.90.
SUNDAYS 6th APRIL & 13th JULY 11am - 5pm
40% to The Gardens Fund of The National Trust for Scotland
For other opening details see page 133

HEXAGON HOUSE, Bardowie &
(Mr & Mrs John Thomson)
A lochside one acre garden created over the last few years. Small woodland area and varied planting of interesting trees, shrubs and plants. Teas. Plant stall. Route: A807 Torrance/Milngavie. In Bardowie take A81 to Strathblane 100 yards. Turn left into parking area. Proceed on foot 500 yards down castle drive. Parking for disabled only at house. No dogs please. ·
Admission £1.00 Children over 12 50p
SUNDAY 8th JUNE 2 - 5pm
40% to the Church of St James the Less, Bishopbriggs

INVERMAY, 48 Wellshot Drive, Cambuslang
(Mrs M Robertson)
A plant lovers' garden. Wide variety of unusual bulbs, rock plants, herbaceous plants, shrubs (many named) in a very sheltered, suburban garden. Greenhouse with fuchsias. Something in flower all through the year - a special town garden. Teas. Plant Stall. A730 (East Kilbride) or A749/A724 (Hamilton) from Glasgow. Convenient to M74/M73. Wellshot Drive starts at back of Cambuslang station.
Admission £1.50 Children over 12 50p
APRIL to SEPTEMBER   Visitors welcome, please telephone first: 0141 641 1632
40% to Children First

KITTOCH MILL, Carmunnock
(Brigadier & Mrs Howard Jordan)
This waterside and woodland garden contains the National Collection of Hostas in Scotland with over 300 varieties growing in different conditions. Many varieties and species of ligularia are planted out on the river banks and woodland areas. A Japanese-style garden, close to the house featuring a Yatsu-Hashi (zig-zag bridge), leads the visitor over a lacquered bridge into the woodland area. Many other unusual plants are to be seen and the garden is a haven for native flora and fauna. Plant stall with many gems from the garden. Please - no dogs. Situated off B759 Busby/Carmunnock. Parking is allowed on far side of road.
Admission £1.00
SUNDAY 6th JULY 2 - 5pm
40% to N C C P G (Strathclyde)

WHITEMOSS HOUSE, East Kilbride
(Mr & Mrs Albert Heasman)
A garden of about one acre, developed over the last 25 years but also containing mature beech, chestnut and sycamore trees. The mixed borders and small woodland garden include a variety of acid loving shrubs and perennials mostly grown from seed or cuttings. During the past winter the layout has been developed to include a small burn and a new island bed. Teas. Plant stall. In Whitemoss Recreation Area opposite bowling greens and tennis courts. Enter via the John Wright Sports Centre car park, Calderwood Road and follow signs.
Admission £1.00 Children over 12 50p
SUNDAY 10th AUGUST 2 - 5pm
40% to East Kilbride & District Hospice Care Appeal

S G S PLANT SALE
Kilmardinny House Arts Centre, 50 Kilmardinny Avenue, Bearsden
SATURDAY 13th SEPTEMBER 11 - 4pm
Admission free. Good parking facilities. Signed from A81 Strathblane road.
All takings to Scotland's Gardens Scheme.

ISLE OF ARRAN

District Organiser:	**Mrs S C Gibbs,** Dougarie, Isle of Arran KA27 8EB
Hon. Treasurer:	**Mr J Hill,** Bank of Scotland, Brodick, Isle of Arran KA27 8AL

DATES OF OPENING

Dougarie	Sunday 29 June	2 - 5pm
Brodick Castle & Country Park	Wednesday 9 July	10am – 5pm
Brodick Castle & Country Park	Wednesday 6 August	10am – 5pm

BRODICK CASTLE & COUNTRY PARK (mostly)
(The National Trust for Scotland)
Semi-tropical plants and shrubs. Walled garden. Rock garden. Free guided walks. Car park free. Morning coffee, lunch and tea available in Castle. NTS shop. Brodick 2 miles. Service buses from Brodick Pier to Castle. Regular sailings from Ardrossan and from Claonaig (Argyll). Information from Caledonian MacBrayne, Gourock.
Tel: 01475 33755.
Admission to Garden & Country Park £2.30. Children & OAPs £1.50
WEDNESDAYS 9th JULY and 6th AUGUST 10 am - 5 pm
40% to The Gardens Fund of the National Trust for Scotland
For other opening details see page 123

DOUGARIE
(Mr & Mrs S C Gibbs)
Terraced garden in castellated folly. Shrubs, herbaceous borders, traditional kitchen garden. Tea. Produce stall. Blackwaterfoot 5 miles. Regular ferry sailing from Ardrossan and from Claonaig (Argyll). Information from Caledonian MacBrayne, Gourock. Tel: 01475 337355.
Admission £1.00 Children 50p
SUNDAY 29th JUNE 2 - 5pm
40% to Isle of Arran Hospital Supporters' League

KINCARDINE & DEESIDE

District Organiser: **Mrs J Mackie,** Bent, Laurencekirk AB30 1EA

Area Organisers: **The Hon Mrs J K O Arbuthnott,** Kilternan, Arbuthnott, Laurencekirk AB30 1NA

Mrs E H Hartwell, Burnigill, Burnside, Fettercairn AB30 1XX

Dr Frances McCance, House of Strachan, Strachan Banchory AB31 3NN

Hon. Treasurer: **Mr D S Gauld,** 18 Reed Crescent, Laurencekirk AB30 1EF

DATES OF OPENING

Shooting Greens, Strachan .... 27 April – 12 May by arrangement

Shooting Greens, Strachan .... Sunday 27 April   2 – 5pm
Drum Castle, Drumoak .... Sunday 18 May   1.30 – 5pm
The Burn House &
    The Burn Garden House, Glenesk .... Sunday 1 June   2 - 5pm
Inchmarlo House Garden, Banchory .... Sunday 1 June   1.30-5pm

Crathes Castle, Banchory	Sunday 22 June	2 – 5pm
Glassel Lodge, Banchory	Sunday 13 July	2 - 5pm
House of Strachan, Banchory	Sunday 20 July	2 - 5pm
Douneside House, Tarland	Sunday 27 July	2 – 5pm
Glenbervie House, Drumlithie	Sunday 27 July	2 – 5pm
Balmanno, Marykirk	Sunday 3 August	2 – 5.30pm

BALMANNO, Marykirk, by Laurencekirk ♿ (gravel paths)
(Mr & Mrs Ronald Simson)
A traditional Scottish 18th century walled garden with flower borders and vegetable plots. Splendid views of the Grampians. Home baked teas. Plant stall. Balmanno is three-quarters of a mile north of Marykirk. Turn right at unmarked crossroads, up hill a few hundred yards on right.
Admission £1.50 Children 50p
SUNDAY 3rd AUGUST 2 - 5.30 pm
20% to Macmillan Cancer Ward, Stracathro Hospital   20% to Marykirk Hall Fund

---

THE BURN HOUSE & THE BURN GARDEN HOUSE, Glenesk ♿ (no toilet facility)
(London Goodenough Trust for Overseas Graduates)
The Burn House built in 1790. Grounds of 190 acres including 2½ mile river path by River North Esk. Tea in Mansion House. Route: Edzell 1 mile. Front gate situated on north side of River North Esk bridge on B966.
Admission £1.50 Children 75p
SUNDAY 1st JUNE 2 - 5pm
20% to Gardeners' Royal Benevolent Society   20% to Army Benevolent Fund

---

CRATHES CASTLE, Banchory ♿
(The National Trust for Scotland)
Walled gardens (3.75 acres) containing eight distinct and separate gardens, including magnificent yew hedges planted in 1702, rare shrubs and fine herbaceous borders. All combine to form the finest patterned garden in northern Scotland. Extensive wild gardens and grounds containing adventure playground, picnic areas and some 10 miles of marked trails. Exhibitions, shop and licensed restaurant. Sale of plants, garden walks, ranger walks, forest walks. Situated off A93, 3 miles east of Banchory, 15 miles west of Aberdeen.
Admission quoted includes castle, garden, estate and use of all facilities. A timed entry system to the castle applies to all visitors to avoid overcrowding in smaller rooms but there is no restriction on time spent inside. Castle tickets can be obtained on arrival.
Admission (combined ticket) £4.50 Children & OAPs £3.00
SUNDAY 22nd JUNE 2 - 5 pm
40% to The Gardens Fund of The National Trust for Scotland
For other opening details see page 124

DOUNESIDE HOUSE, Tarland &

(The MacRobert Trusts)

Ornamental and rose gardens around a large lawn with uninterrupted views to the Deeside Hills and Grampians; large, well-stocked vegetable garden, beech walks and water gardens. Cars free. Tea in house. Plant stall. Ballater and District Pipe Band. Tarland 1½ miles. Route: B9119 towards Aberdeen.

Admission £1.50 Children & OAPs £1.00

SUNDAY 27th JULY 2 - 5 pm

40% to Gardeners' Royal Benevolent Society (Netherbyres Appeal)

DRUM CASTLE, Drumoak, by Banchory &

(The National Trust for Scotland)

Walled garden of historic roses, opened June 1991. Roses representing 17th to 20th centuries at their best in mid-June to mid-July. Grounds contain arboretum, woodland walk, picnic area and farmland walk. Marquee teas. Plant and flower sale. Maypole Dancing. Special activities for children including Spring Bonnet competition and Treasure Hunt. Route: 10 miles west of Aberdeen and 8 miles east of Banchory on A93. Garden & Grounds only £1.80   OAPs & children £1.20

Castle supplement £2.20   Children £1.50 Family ticket £4.80

SUNDAY 18th MAY 1.30 - 5 pm

40% to The Gardens Fund of The National Trust for Scotland

For other opening details see page 133

GLASSEL LODGE, Banchory &

(Mr & Mrs M Welsh)

A developing garden containing flowers, kitchen garden and woodland. Plant stall. 4 miles from A93 west of Banchory take right turn marked Glassel, Torphins,Lumphanan. Admission £1.50 Children 50p

SUNDAY 13th JULY 2 - 5pm

40% to Friends of Cruickshank Botanic Garden

GLENBERVIE HOUSE, Drumlithie, Stonehaven

(Mrs C S Macphie)

Nucleus of present day house dates from the 15th century. Additions in 17th and 19th centuries. Walled garden with fine herbaceous and annual borders. Ornamental conservatory contains a dazzling display of interesting plants, also woodland garden. Teas. Plant and baking stalls. Drumlithie 1 mile. Garden 1½ miles off A90. NOT SUITABLE FOR WHEELCHAIRS.

Admission £1.75 Children 80p Cars free

SUNDAY 27th JULY 2 - 5 pm

40% to West Mearns Parish Church

HOUSE OF STRACHAN, Strachan, Banchory

(Dr F McCance)

A mature garden of two acres, the grounds of what was Strachan Manse. It slopes south to the River Feugh and has a variety of roses, herbaceous borders and other plants and shrubs. Teas. Plant stall. On B976 on south side in centre of village of Strachan. Admission £1.50

SUNDAY 20th JULY 2 - 5pm

40% to Friends of Crossroads

INCHMARLO HOUSE GARDEN, Banchory   ♿ (limited)
(Skene Enterprises (Aberdeen) Ltd)
An ever changing 5 acre woodland garden, originally planted in the early Victorian era, featuring ancient Scots pines, Douglas firs, yews, beeches and a variety of other trees which form a dramatic background to an early summer riot of mature azaleas and rhododendrons producing a splendour of colour and scents.
Tea, coffee, homebakes - £2.00. From Aberdeen via North Deeside Road on A93 1m west of Banchory, turn right at main gate to Inchmarlo House.
Admission £2.00 Children free
SUNDAY 1st JUNE 1.30 - 5pm
40% to British Heart Foundation

SHOOTING GREENS, Strachan, Banchory ♿ (limited access)
(Mr & Mrs Donald Stuart-Hamilton)
Medium sized garden, landscaped with local stone, stems from terracing rough moorland near a burn and woodland glen. Short vistas and distant Grampian hills back raised, mixed, erica and alpine beds. Row of cairns and two small amphitheatres. Beyond a small orchard, sloping to ponds, lie short walks by burn and through mixed and beech groves, one to a view point. Forestry Commission walks nearby. CARS PLEASE PARK ALONG PUBLIC ROAD. Route: On east side, near top of north-south Deeside link road between Potarch Hotel (2½m) and Feughside Inn (1m) white stones at drive end; approximately 300 metres from car park for Forestry Commission's own Shooting Greens walks.
Admission £1.50 Children 50p
SUNDAY 27th APRIL 2 - 5 pm.   To 12th May by arrangement. Tel: 01330 850221.
40% to St Thomas's Church, Aboyne

LOCHABER, BADENOCH & STRATHSPEY

Joint District Organisers:	**Mrs J Drysdale,** Ralia, Newtonmore PH20 1BD
	Mrs J Ramsden, Dalchully, Laggan PH20 1BU
Hon. Treasurer:	**Mrs J Drysdale**

DATES OF OPENING

Ardtornish, Lochaline	Sunday 25 May	2 – 6pm
Achnacarry, Spean Bridge	Sunday 25 May	2 - 5.30pm
Ard-Daraich, Ardgour	Sunday 1 June	2 - 5pm
Allt a' Mhuilin & Riverside, Spean Bridge	Sunday 8 June	2 - 5.30pm
Aberarder, Kinlochlaggan	Sunday 21 September	2 – 5.30pm
Ardverikie, Kinlochlaggan	Sunday 21 September	2 – 5.30pm

ABERARDER, Kinlochlaggan
(Lady Feilden)
Flower and kitchen garden. Marvellous views down Loch Laggan. Plant stall.
On A86 between Newtonmore and Spean Bridge at east end of Loch Laggan.
Combined admission with Ardverikie £2.00. Children under 12 free
SUNDAY 21st SEPTEMBER 2 - 5.30 pm
40% to Cancer Relief Macmillan Fund

ACHNACARRY, Spean Bridge &
(Sir Donald & Lady Cameron of Lochiel)
An interesting wild garden in a lovely setting with a profusion of rhododendrons,
azaleas and flowers along the banks of the River Arkaig. A fine Georgian house full of
history. Clan Cameron Museum. Forest walks. Flower stall. Teas in Village Hall 200
yards from the house. Route: A82 Spean Bridge; left at Commando Memorial marked
Gairlochy. At Gairlochy turn right off B8005. Achnacarry is 7 miles from Spean Bridge.
Admission: House & garden £2.00 Children 50p.
SUNDAY 25th MAY 2 - 5.30pm
40% to Multiple Sclerosis Society (Lochaber)

ALLT a' MHUILINN, Spean Bridge
(Mr & Mrs Gary Roady)
An attractive sloping riverside garden. Herbaceous border and shrubs. Fine oak and
beech trees. Riverside and azalea walks. Parking at Little Chef, Spean Bridge. Route:
Allt a' Mhuillin lies diagonally across the road (to left) from Little Chef car park.
JOINT OPENING WITH RIVERSIDE, INVERGLOY.
Admission £2.00 Children over 14 and OAPs £1.00, includes both gardens.
SUNDAY 8th JUNE 2 - 5.30pm
40% to Save the Children Fund

ARD-DARAICH, Ardgour, by Fort William
(Major David & Lady Edith Maclaren)
Seven acre hill garden, in a spectacular setting, with many fine and uncommon
rhododendrons, an interesting selection of trees and shrubs and a large collection of
camellias, acers and sorbus. Home made teas in house. Cake and plant stall. Route:
west from Fort William, across the Corran Ferry and a mile on the right further west.
Admission £1.50 Children & OAPs 50p
SUNDAY 1st JUNE 2 - 5pm
40% to Multiple Sclerosis Society (Fort William branch)

ARDTORNISH, Lochaline, Morvern
(Mrs John Raven)
Garden of interesting mature conifers, rhododendrons, deciduous trees and shrubs set
set amidst magnificent scenery. Home made teas in main house 2 - 5pm. Route A884.
Lochaline 3 miles.
Admission £2.00 Children free OAPs £1.00
SUNDAY 25th MAY 2 - 6pm
40% to Morvern Parish Church

ARDVERIKIE, Kinlochlaggan ♿
(Mrs P Laing & Mrs E T Smyth Osbourne)
Lovely setting on Loch Laggan with magnificent trees. Walled garden with large
collection of acers, shrubs and herbaceous. Architecturally interesting house. On A86
between Newtonmore and Spean Bridge - entrance at east end of Loch Laggan, by gate
lodge over bridge. Home made teas.
Combined admission with Aberarder £2.00 Children under 12 free
SUNDAY 21st SEPTEMBER 2 - 5.30 pm
40% to Cancer Relief Macmillan Fund

 # RIVERSIDE, Invergloy
(Mr & Mrs David Bennet)
A redeveloped portion of a once-famous garden. Fine old trees surround the collection
of rhododendrons, acers and flowers. Not suitable for wheelchairs. Please park at The
Coach House, Glenfintaig, from where a shuttle car service will operate. Route: 4 miles
NE of Spean Bridge on A82, The Coach House car park is on the right. Teas at The
Coach House at commercial rates. JOINT OPENING WITH ALLT a' MHUILINN,
SPEAN BRIDGE.
Admission £2.00 Children over 14 & OAPs £1.00, includes both gardens.
SUNDAY 8th JUNE 2 - 5.30pm
40% to Save the Children Fund

MIDLOTHIAN

District Organiser:	**The Hon Mrs C J Dalrymple,** OBE, Oxenfoord Mains, Dalkeith EH22 2PF
Area Organisers:	**Mrs George Burnet,** Rose Court, Inveresk
	Mrs S MacMillan, Beechpark House, Broomieknowe, Lasswade EH18 1LN
Joint Hon. Treasurers:	**The Hon Mrs C J Dalrymple,** OBE
	Cmdr H Faulkner, Currie Lea, Pathhead EH37 5XB

DATES OF OPENING

Arniston, Gorebridge	Tuesdays, Thursdays & Sundays	
	July – mid-September	
Greenfield Lodge, Lasswade	First Tuesday of each month	
	March-September incl. 2 - 5pm	
	All year, by appointment	
The Mill House, Temple	Second Wednesday of each month	
	April-September incl. 2 - 5pm	
Newhall, Carlops	Tuesday to Thursdays, April - October	
	Glen 1 - 5pm. Walled garden 2 - 5pm.	

Prestonhall, Pathhead	Sunday 16 March	2 – 5pm
Greenfield Lodge, Lasswade	Tuesday 25 March	2 – 5pm
Prestonhall, Pathhead	Sunday 20 April	2 – 6pm
Oxenfoord Castle, Pathhead	Sunday 27 April	2 - 5.30pm
Newhall, Carlops	Sunday 4 May	2 – 5pm
Arniston, Gorebridge	Sunday 11 May	2 – 5pm
Lasswade: Broomieknowe	Sat & Sun 28/29 June	2 – 5pm
Oxenfoord Mains, Dalkeith	Sunday 6 July	2 - 6pm
Lasswade: Kevock Road	Sat & Sun 12/13 July	2 - 5pm
Newhall, Carlops	Sunday 3 August	2 - 6pm
Carberry Tower, Musselburgh	Sunday 28 September	2 - 5.30pm
SGS Plant Sale, Oxenfoord Mains,Dalkeith	Sunday 12 October	10.30am -3pm

ARNISTON, Gorebridge ✦ (partly)
(Mrs Aedrian Dundas-Bekker)
William Adam Mansion House. Parklands. Sunken garden which was laid out in the late 18th century with bridges incorporating stones from old Parliament House. Tour of House £2.50 Teas. Route: B6372, Temple direction. Gorebridge 2 miles.
Admission 50p Children 25p
TUESDAYS, THURSDAYS & SUNDAYS from JULY to Mid-SEPTEMBER 2 - 5pm
Groups by appointment throughout rest of year. Tel: 01875 830238
SUNDAY 11th MAY 2 - 5pm
40% to The National Trust for Scotland, Newhailes Appeal

CARBERRY TOWER, Musselburgh ✦
(Church of Scotland)
Gracious estate wih magnificent trees. Laid out by the Elphinstones, a dendrologist's delight. Formal sunken rose garden, designed by Osgood Mackenzie and gifted by the Queen Mother. Baronial mansion with Georgian features, the tower dating from the 15th century. Award winning Mary Ross Chapel. Guided tree walks. Plant stall. Teas with home baking, charged at counter. Chapel service at 5pm. Dogs outside only and on lead please. Route: A6124, one mile south of Inveresk. From Edinburgh take Wallyford A6094 exit off A1, follow signs. From Haddington, take Dalkeith A6094 exit. Admission to house and garden £2.00 Children free
SUNDAY 28th SEPTEMBER 2 - 5.30pm
40% to Friends of Carberry

GREENFIELD LODGE, Lasswade &

(Alan & Helen Dickinson)

A 1½ acre wooded garden with a very wide range of flowering shrubs, unusual herbaceous plants, ornamental grasses, alpines and bulbs, including the National Chionodoxa Collection. The garden is designed to give colour and interest throughout the year: hellebores, cyclamen, aquilegias, meconopsis, eryngiums, dieramas and gentians are well represented. Early 19th century bow-fronted house with later additions (not open). Plant stall. Parking. No dogs please. Off the Loanhead to Lasswade road (A768) at the end of Green Lane, which is off Church Road. Admission £1.50 Careful children free.

First Tuesday of each month MARCH—SEPTEMBER incl. 2 - 5pm
TUESDAY 25th MARCH 2 - 5pm
and throughout the year by appt., tel. 0131 663 9338 day before proposed visit.
40% to Shelter (Scotland)

LASSWADE: Broomieknowe

Rose Cottage	Small courtyard with a variety of pot plants.
Gordon Bank	Small cottage garden designed for easy management.
Beechpark House	Flower arranger's garden, informally laid out for interesting plants, flowering evergreen shrubs for all year round cutting.
Mount Ceres	Featuring small gardens within the whole: herb, heather, fern, rose, herbaceous and woodland areas, ponds, stream, pergolas and many unusual plants.
The Hill	A landscaped hillside garden with fine views over a wooded valley to the Pentland hills. Many varieties of heaths, heathers and conifers, small natural stone water features, indoor fuchsias.
Fermain	One-third acre with oriental and continental touches with natural and formal ponds.

Teas. Plant stalls.
Admission £2.00 OAPs 50p
SATURDAY & SUNDAY 28th & 29th JUNE 2 - 5pm
40% to Local Charities

LASSWADE: Kevock Road & (in part)
No. 4	Mrs J Abel
No. 14	Professor & Mrs G Craig
No. 16	Professor & Mrs D Rankin

Kevock is a conservation area on the bank of the River Esk with attractive views of the valley and mature woodland. Each garden has a distinctive character, some of the land being flat, some sloping. They contain a wide range of mature trees, shrubs, especially rhododendrons and roses, primulas, alpines and heathers. Plant stall. Teas on Sunday. Route: A768 runs between Loanhead and Lasswade; Kevock Road lies to the south and is indicated by a sign for the stables.
Admission £2.00 includes all gardens Children free
SATURDAY & SUNDAY 12th & 13th JULY 2 - 5pm
40% to Sense (Scotland)

THE MILL HOUSE, Temple
(Mrs C F Yannaghas)

A charming riverside garden with botanical interest throughout the year, including spring flowers, camomile lawn and interesting use of ground cover. A conservation area within Knights Templar enclave. Cream teas. Temple is 3 miles off A7 on B6372. Admission £1.50

The second WEDNESDAY of each month APRIL - SEPTEMBER 2 - 5pm

40% to Children First

NEWHALL, Carlops   ♿ (Walled garden only)
(Robert Hardy CBE and The Orcome Trust)

Scene of Allan Ramsay's celebrated dramatic poem 'The Gentle Shepherd' and meeting place of the "Worthies", his patrons; glen of the North Esk with "Habbie's How", "Peggy's Pool" and "Craigie Bield". Parkland. Traditional 18th century Scottish walled garden; spring bulbs; mixed borders; shrubs; kitchen garden; lily pool; vine house with sturdy and aged vines. Teas. Some pot plants for sale at August opening. **Sorry no dogs.** On A702 Edinburgh/Biggar, exactly half mile after Ninemileburn and 1 mile before Carlops. Gates on left.

APRIL to OCTOBER, Tuesdays, Wednesdays & Thursdays.

Glen: 1 - 5pm; Walled Garden: 2 - 5pm

SUNDAY 4th MAY 2 - 5pm Admission £1.50 Children 50p

SUNDAY 3rd AUGUST 2 - 6pm Admission £2.00 Children 50p

40% to Childrens Hospice Association Scotland

OXENFOORD CASTLE, near Pathhead   ♿ (partly)
(The Hon Michael Dalrymple)

Extensive grounds with masses of daffodils, some early rhododendrons and new development in sunken garden. The house has been recently renovated and will be open for teas. Route: A68. Opposite Gorebridge turning ¾ mile north of Pathhead. Admission £1.50

SUNDAY 27th APRIL 2 - 5.30pm

40% to The Royal Hospital for Sick Children

OXENFOORD MAINS, Dalkeith   ♿
(Major Hon Colin & Mrs Dalrymple)

A small garden of old fashioned roses, mixed shrubs and ground cover. Interesting development from a field in the last 30 years. Plant stall. Strawberry teas. No dogs please. Route: 4 miles south of Dalkeith on A68, turn left for 1 mile on A6093. Admission £1.50 Children free

SUNDAY 6th JULY 2 - 6pm

40% to Cranstoun Church

PRESTONHALL, Pathhead   ♿
(Major & Mrs J H Callander)
Set in extensive parkland originally laid out in the 18th century. The mature park trees with their surrounding woodland and wild gardens are a wonderful setting for carpets of snowdrops in March and a profusion of daffodils and rhododendrons in April/May. Many new species of trees have been planted recently. Signed off A68 at Pathhead 25 minutes south east of Edinburgh.
Admission £2.00 (£1.50 in March) Children & OAPs £1.50 (£1.00 in March)
SUNDAY 16th MARCH 2 - 5pm
SUNDAY 20th APRIL 2 - 6pm
20% to Malcolm Sargent Cancer Fund for Children
20% to Crichton Collegiate Church Trust

SGS PLANT SALE
A Bring and Buy Plant Sale will be held at Oxenfoord Mains, Dalkeith, on
SUNDAY 12th OCTOBER 10.30am - 3pm.
Route: 4 miles south of Dalkeith on A68, turn left for one mile on A6093.
Admission free.

Good at photography?
Details of our photographic competition are opposite page 65

MORAY & NAIRN

District Organiser:	**Mrs H D P Brown,** Tilliedivie House, Relugas, Dunphail, Forres IV36 0QL
Hon. Treasurer:	**Mr H D P Brown,** Tilliedivie House, Relugas, Dunphail, Forres IV36 0QL

DATES OF OPENING

Carestown Steading, Deskford	Sunday 8 June	2 - 5pm
Delnesmuir, Nairn	Sunday 8 June	2 - 5pm
Glen Grant Distillery Garden, near Elgin	Saturday 14 June	9.30am - 5pm
Gordonstoun, Duffus	Sunday 22 June	2 - 5.30pm
Drummuir Castle Garden, by Keith	Sunday 20 July	2 - 5pm

CARESTOWN STEADING, Deskford, Buckie
(Rora Paglieri)
An award winning steading conversion in a three acre rural garden reclaimed from wasteland in 1990 and still developing and maturing. The plants and flowers are native as far as possible and the few exotics have been present in Scotland for many years. The aim is for the gardens to look natural. The one example of manicured gardening is the 90 sq m. of courtyard with knot beds of box in the old Scottish tradition. Vegetable garden, orchard and ponds. Teas by local Guides. Plant stall. Route: East off B9018 Cullen/Keith (Cullen 3m, Keith 9½ m). Follow SGS signs towards Milton and Carestown.
Admission £1.50 Children 50p
SUNDAY 8th JUNE 2 - 5pm
All takings to Scotland's Gardens Scheme

DELNESMUIR, Nairn
(Mrs F J Macgillivray)
Woodland walk. Rhododendrons, azaleas. Well-kept lawns and shrubbery. Teas £1.50. Stalls. Entrance off A96 Inverness road, 1 mile west of Nairn.
Admission £1.00 Children 50p
SUNDAY 8th JUNE 2 - 5 pm
40% to Barnardos

DRUMMUIR CASTLE GARDEN, by Keith
(Mr & Mrs Alex Gordon-Duff)
Traditional walled garden using organic methods to grow fruit, vegetables and herbs. Plant stall. Teas and ice cream. Five miles from Keith and Dufftown on B9014.
Admission £1.50 Children under 12 free
SUNDAY 20th JULY 2 - 5pm
40% to Drummuir Community Association

GLEN GRANT DISTILLERY GARDEN, Rothes, near Elgin ♿ (partly)
(The Chivas and Glenlivet Group)
An award-winning restoration of this delightful Victorian garden created in the glen behind Glen Grant Distillery by Major James Grant, the owner of the distillery. The woodland setting of the enchanting informal garden has been carefully restored to its original Victorian glory. Old woodland walks and log bridges have been rebuilt, the lily pond restored and the lovely mature orchards and rhododendrons have come back into view. The ornamental areas have been replanted with native specimens and plants from America, China and the Himalayas. A visit to the distillery and garden includes exhibitions, audio-visual show about the life of Major Grant and a free dram of Glen Grant pure malt Scotch whisky, which you can choose to enjoy at Major Grant's Dram Pavilion up in the garden if you wish. Route: On A941 Grantown-on-Spey road at north end of Rothes, about 10 miles south of Elgin.
Admission £2.50 Under 18 free
SATURDAY 14th JUNE 9.30am - 5pm
40% to Grant Hall, Rothes

GORDONSTOUN, Duffus, near Elgin ♿
(The Headmaster, Gordonstoun School)
School grounds; Gordonstoun House (Georgian House of 1775/6 incorporating earlier 17th century house built for 1st Marquis of Huntly) and School Chapel - both open. Unique circle of former farm buildings known as the Round Square. Teas. Entrance off B9012 4 miles from Elgin at Duffus village.
Admission £1.50 Children 50p
SUNDAY 22nd JUNE 2 - 5.30pm
All takings to Scotland's Gardens Scheme

PERTH & KINROSS

Joint District Organisers:	**Mrs M E Hamilton,** Glencarse House, Glencarse PH2 7LF
	Mrs Charles Moncrieff, Easter Elcho, Rhynd PH2 8QQ
Area Organisers:	**Mrs D J W Anstice,** Broomhill, Abernethy PH2 9LQ
	Mrs C Dunphie, Wester Cloquhat, Bridge of Cally PH10 7JP
	Mrs T J Hope Thomson, High Birches, Fairmount Road, Perth PH2 7AW
	Mrs Alastair Leslie, Seasyde House, Errol PH2 7TA
	Lady Livesay, Crosshill House, Strathallan, Auchterarder PH3 7LN
	Mrs Colin Maitland Dougall, Dowhill, Kelty, Fife KY4 0HZ
	The Hon Mrs Ranald Noel Paton, Easter Dunbarnie, Bridge of Earn PH2 9ED
	Mrs Athel Price, Urlar Farm, Aberfeldy PH15 2EW
Hon. Treasurer:	**Mrs J Bell,** Greenwood, Kinfauns, Perth PH2 7JZ

DATES OF OPENING

Ardvorlich, Lochearnhead	11 May - 8 June	2 - 6pm
Bolfracks, Aberfeldy	Daily 28 March – 31 October	10am – 6pm
Cluny House, Aberfeldy	Daily 1 March – 31 October	10am – 6pm
Drummond Castle Gardens, Muthill ..	Daily May - October 2 - 6pm (last entrance 5pm)	
Lude, Blair Atholl	20 June – 6 August by appt.	
Scone Palace, Perth	28 March – 13 October	9.30am – 5pm
Meikleour House, by Blairgowrie	Sunday 13 April	2 - 5pm
Glendoick, by Perth	Sunday 4 May	2 – 5pm
Branklyn, Perth	Sunday 11 May	9.30am – sunset
Meikleour House, by Blairgowrie	Sunday 11 May	2 - 5pm

Glendoick, by Perth	Sunday 18 May	2 – 5pm
Bonskeid House, near Pitlochry	Sat&Sun 24/25 May	11am-5pm
Easter Dunbarnie, Bridge of Earn	Sunday 25 May	2 - 6pm
Kennacoil House, Dunkeld	Sunday 1 June	2 – 6pm
Damside, Auchterarder..	Sunday 8 June	2 - 6pm
Meikleour House, by Blairgowrie	Sunday 8 June	2 - 5pm
Branklyn, Perth	Sunday 15 June	9.30am – sunset
Cloquhat Gardens, Bridge of Cally	Sunday 15 June	2 – 6pm
Dowhill, Cleish..	Sunday 15 June	2 - 5pm
Nye Cottage, Knapp, Inchture	Sunday 29 June	2 - 5pm
Rowanlea & Shian, Birnam	Sunday 6 July	2 - 5pm
Damside, Auchterarder...	Sunday 20 July	2 - 6pm
Wester Dalqueich, Carnbo	Wednesday 23 July	2 - 5pm
Wester Dalqueich, Carnbo	Wednesday 30 July	2 - 5pm
Drummond Castle Gardens, Muthill	Sunday 3 August	2 – 6pm
Wester Dalqueich, Carnbo	Wednesday 6 August	2 - 5pm
Blairgowrie & Rattray Gardens	Sunday 10 August	1 – 6pm
Cluniemore, Pitlochry	Sunday 10 August	2 – 5pm
Megginch Castle, Errol	Sunday 10 August	2 – 5pm
Wester Dalqueich, Carnbo	Wednesday 13 August	2 - 5pm
Bonskeid House, near Pitlochry	Sat&Sun 20/21 September	11am-5pm
Meikleour House, by Blairgowrie	Sunday 19 October	2 - 5pm

ARDVORLICH, Lochearnhead

(Mr & Mrs Sandy Stewart)
Beautiful glen with rhododendrons (species and many hybrids) grown in wild conditions amid oaks and birches. Gum boots advisable when wet.
On south Lochearn road 3m from Lochearnhead, 4½ m from St Fillans.
Admission £1.50 Children under 12 free
11th MAY to 8th JUNE incl. 2 - 6pm
40% to St Columba's Hospice

BLAIRGOWRIE & RATTRAY ঌ (partly)

The "Blair in Bloom" Committee would like to invite you to visit some colourful prizewinning town gardens of varying sizes. Teas and Plant Stalls. Maps and tickets available from the Tourist Information Centre, Wellmeadow, Blairgowrie. No dogs, except guide dogs, please.
Admission £2.00 Accompanied children under 12 free
SUNDAY 10th AUGUST 1 - 6pm
40% to Local Registered Charities

BOLFRACKS, Aberfeldy

(Mr J D Hutchison CBE)
Garden overlooking the Tay valley. Walled garden with borders of trees, shrubs and perennials. Burn garden with rhododendrons, azaleas, primulas, meconopsis, etc. in woodland setting. Masses of bulbs in spring. Good autumn colour. No dogs please. Limited range of plants for sale. Route: 2 miles west of Aberfeldy on A827. White gates and Lodge on left of road. Not suitable for wheelchairs.
Admission £2.00 Children under 16 free
DAILY 28th MARCH to 31st OCTOBER 10 am - 6 pm
Donation to Scotland's Gardens Scheme

95

BONSKEID HOUSE, near Pitlochry
(YMCA Scottish National Council)
The house, formerly the property of George Freeland Barbour, has been run as a holiday and conference centre by the YMCA since 1921. The house and grounds (38 acres) were sited in 1800 by Alexander Stewart to take advantage of the dramatic views across the River Tummel, and for visitors to experience the romanticism of a baronial residence in a wild woodland setting. Woodland walks, some steep paths, wandering amongst mature exotic specimen trees and ponticum rhododendrons. After suffering many years of neglect, the grounds have now benefited from 24 months of an ongoing reclamation project. Flower beds under construction, walled garden reclaimed, rare breed animals and birds, lovely autumn colours. Ranger service. Teas. Route: A9 Killiecrankie exit, 4 miles along B8019 Tummel Bridge road, on left hand side.
Admission £1.50 Children 50p
SATURDAY & SUNDAY 24th& 25th MAY 11am - 5pm
SATURDAY & SUNDAY 20th & 21st SEPTEMBER 11am - 5pm
20% to YMCA   20% to the Scottish Wildlife Trust

BRANKLYN, Perth
(The National Trust for Scotland)
Rhododendrons, alpines, herbaceous and peat garden plants from all over the world. Cars free. Tea and coffee. On A85 Perth/Dundee road.
Admission £2.30 Children & OAPs £1.50
SUNDAY 11th MAY and SUNDAY 15th JUNE   9.30 am - sunset
40% to The Gardens Fund of The National Trust for Scotland
For other opening details see page 122

CLOQUHAT GARDENS, Bridge of Cally ⅃ (partly)
Cloquhat. (Colonel Peter Dunphie CBE)
Fine views down to river. Azaleas, rhododendrons, shrubs. Woodland and burnside gardens. Terrace with rock plants. Walled garden.
Wester Cloquhat. (Brigadier & Mrs Christopher Dunphie)
Small garden started in 1989. Splendid situation. Several mixed borders with wide variety of shrubs and herbaceous plants. Heather bank. Teas and plant stall. No dogs please. Turn off A93 just north of Bridge of Cally and follow yellow signs one mile.
Admission to both gardens £2.00 Children 50p
SUNDAY 15th JUNE 2 - 6 pm
40% to SSAFA

CLUNIEMORE, Pitlochry ⅃
(Major Sir David & Lady Butter)
Water garden, rock garden. Woodlands in beautiful setting. Shrubs, herbaceous borders, annual border and roses. Plant stall. Tea, biscuits and ice cream. Parties by appointment any time. On A9 Pitlochry bypass.
Admission £2.00 Children under 16 free
SUNDAY 10th AUGUST 2 - 5pm
40% to The Pushkin Prizes in Scotland

CLUNY HOUSE, Aberfeldy
(Mr J & Mrs W Mattingley)

Woodland garden with many specimen trees, shrubs and rhododendrons, with extensive views of Strathtay to Ben Lawers. An outstanding collection of primulas, meconopsis, nomocharis, cardiocrinums and other Himalayan plants. Autumn colour. Plant stall. No dogs please. 3½ miles from Aberfeldy on Weem to Strathtay road.

Admission £2.00 Children under 16 free

DAILY 1st MARCH to 31st OCTOBER 10 am - 6 pm

Donation to Scotland's Gardens Scheme

DAMSIDE, Auchterarder
(Mrs J W G Hume)

Rhododendrons, azaleas, beautiful trees. Shrubs. Home made teas. Plant stall. Situated on old road between Auchterarder and Aberuthven. No dogs please.

Admission £2.00 Children & OAPs £1.00

SUNDAY 8th JUNE 2 - 6pm
SUNDAY 20th JULY 2 - 6pm Garden only. No teas.

20% to Aberuthven Village Hall   20% to Riding for the Disabled

DOWHILL, Cleish
(Mr & Mrs C Maitland Dougall)

Medium sized garden with series of linked ponds. Rhododendrons, primulas and blue poppies in natural setting. Woodland walk to ruins of Dowhill Castle. Teas. Small plant stall. Three-quarters mile off M90, exit 5, towards Crook of Devon.

Admission £2.00 Children 50p

SUNDAY 15th JUNE 2 - 5pm

40% to Cleish Church

DRUMMOND CASTLE GARDENS, Crieff &
(Grimsthorpe & Drummond Castle Trust Ltd)

The gardens of Drummond Castle were originally laid out in 1630 by John Drummond, 2nd Earl of Perth. In 1830 the parterre was changed to an Italian style. One of the most interesting features is the multi-faceted sundial designed by John Mylne, Master Mason to Charles I. The formal garden is said to be one of the finest in Europe and is the largest of its type in Scotland. Open daily May to October 2 - 6 pm (last entrance 5 pm). Entrance 2 miles south of Crieff on Muthill road (A822).

Admission £3.00 OAPs £2.00 Children £1.00

SUNDAY 3rd AUGUST 2 - 6 pm. Teas, raffle, entertainments & stalls.

40% to British Limbless Ex-Servicemen's Association

EASTER DUNBARNIE, Bridge of Earn   &
(The Hon Ranald & Mrs Noel-Paton)

Lovely and surprising six-acre garden, including woodland walks with acers, sorbus, rhododendrons, cardiocrinum giganteum and newly renovated water/quarry garden. Plant stall. Teas. No dogs. Route: 5 minutes from M90 (Exit 9). Take B935 out of Bridge of Earn (Forgandenny road).

Admission £2.00 Children 50p

SUNDAY 25th MAY 2 - 6pm

40% to National Art Collections Fund

GLENDOICK, Perth ♿ (partly)
(Mr & Mrs Peter Cox & family)

Georgian house about 1746 (not open). A lot of replanting in the area by the house is taking place. Walled garden is a mixture of commercial nursery, wall shrubs, trained fruit trees and herbaceous borders. The woodland garden, on the slope above, has meandering paths through the famous rhododendrons and magnolias and many other shrubs and trees. These are complemented by many naturalised herbaceous and wild flowers which make it an enchanting walk. Nursery also open. No dogs please. Refreshments at garden centre 9.30am–5pm. On A90 Perth/Dundee road.

Admission £2.00 Children under 5 free

SUNDAYS 4th & 18th MAY 2 - 5 pm

40% to World Wide Fund for Nature

KENNACOIL HOUSE, Dunkeld
(Mrs Walter Steuart Fothringham)

Informal to wild garden with herbaceous border, shrubs, rhododendrons and azaleas on hillside with exceptional view. Burn with water garden. Teas. Plant stall. No dogs please. Dunkeld 3 miles, off Crieff road A822.

Admission £2.00

SUNDAY 1st JUNE 2 - 6 pm

40% to Leonard Cheshire Homes

LUDE, Blair Atholl ♿
(Mr & Mrs W G Gordon)

A "secret" walled garden built c1815 containing gardens within a garden of trees, peonies, roses and shrubs. Blair Atholl 1¼ miles, entrance is opposite Tilt Hotel.

Admission £2.00

20th JUNE – 6th AUGUST by appointment. Tel: 01796 481240

Donation to Scotland's Gardens Scheme

MEGGINCH CASTLE, Errol ♿
(Captain Drummond of Megginch & Baroness Strange)

15th century turreted castle (not open) with Gothic courtyard and pagoda dovecote. 1,000 year old yews and topiary. Colourful annual border in walled garden. Astrological garden. Home made teas. Plant stall. Memorabilia from "Rob Roy" filmed in the courtyard. Water garden. On A85 between Perth (9½m) and Dundee (12m). Look for Lodge on south side of road.

Admission £2.00 Children free

SUNDAY 10th AUGUST 2 - 5 pm

40% to All Saints Church, Glencarse

MEIKLEOUR HOUSE, by Blairgowrie ♿ (with assistance)
(The Marquis of Lansdowne)

Water and woodland garden on the banks of the River Tay. Fine trees, specie rhododendrons and lovely autumn colours. No dogs please. Entrance to water and woodland garden 300 yards from car parks. Enter via Meikleour Lodge, 5 miles south of Blairgowrie off A93 at its junction with the Stanley/Kinclaven Bridge road.

Admission £1.50 Children free

SUNDAYS 13th APRIL, 11th MAY, 8th JUNE, 19th OCTOBER 2 - 5pm

40% to R N I B (Scotland)

NYE COTTAGE, Knapp, Inchture
(Lt Col & Mrs J A Harrrison)

A two acre garden with many varied walks amongst unusual and interesting trees, old roses, shrubs and herbaceous plants. In the listed village of Knapp, it is a semi-wild , slightly Robinsonian garden developed over the last 15 - 20 years. Not suitable for wheelchairs. Good plant stall. Home baked teas. Turn off A90 at Longforgan, and take the road to Knapp. Signed thereafter.

Admission £2.00 Children £1.00 under 5 free

SUNDAY 29th JUNE 2 - 5pm

20% to Scottish Adoption   20% Abernyte Church

ROWANLEA and SHIAN, Birnam &

Two small gardens, next door to one another and each quite different from the other.
Rowanlea   (Mrs Sheelah Duncan)
A plantsman's delight with close groupings of bulbs, shrubs and herbaceous plants, almost all unusual, and beautifully labelled. The bank at the back of the garden is also planted with many species, creating a semi-wild effect.
Shian (Mr & Mrs Scott Allan)
Planted with interesting trees, chiefly conifers, also many ericas and a stunning display of plants in pots and troughs. Both gardens have a considerable number of clematis and together provide an excellent range of rowans.

Good plant stall. Teas £1.50. No dogs please. Leave A9 by first exit to Birnam from Perth, ½ mile on, pass Shell garage on right , 3rd and 4th bungalows on left after garage.

Admission £1.50 Well behaved children welcomed free

SUNDAY 6th JULY 2 - 5pm

40% to FRAME (Fundraising Association for Medical Equipment)

SCONE PALACE, Perth &
(The Earl of Mansfield)

Extensive and well laid out grounds and a magnificent pinetum dating from 1848; there is a Douglas Fir raised from the original seed sent from America in 1824. The Woodland Garden has attractive walks amongst the rhododendrons and azaleas and leads into the Monks' Playgreen and Friar's Den of the former Abbey of Scone. The Palace of Scone lies adjacent to the Moot Hill where the Kings of Scots were crowned. Full catering by the Palace staff. Adventure playground. Special rates for season tickets and parties. Route A93. Perth 2 miles.

Admission: Palace & Grounds £5.00 Children £2.80 OAPs £4.20 Family £15.00

FRIDAY 28th MARCH to MONDAY 13th OCTOBER 9.30am - 5pm daily

Donation to Scotland's Gardens Scheme

WESTER DALQUEICH, Carnbo   & (partly)
(Mr & Mrs D S Roulston)

Two acre garden by the Ochil Hills, 600ft above sea level. Interesting herbaceous and rock plants, shrubs with informal planting in the glades. Plant stall. No dogs, except guide dogs please. Carnbo village is west of Milnathort. Leave A91 near Carnbo village and travel north for ½ mile.

Admission £2.00

WEDNESDAYS 23rd & 30th JULY, 6th & 13th AUGUST 2 - 5pm
& evenings by arrangement. Large parties please telephone 01577 840229 beforehand.

40% to Strathcarron Hospice, Denny

RENFREW & INVERCLYDE

Joint District Organisers: **Mrs J R Hutton,** Auchenclava, Finlaystone,
Langbank PA14 6TJ

Mrs Daphne Ogg, Nittingshill, Kilmacolm PA13 4SG

Area Organisers: **Lady Denholm,** Newton of Bell Trees, Lochwinnoch PA12 4JL
Mr J Wardrop, St Kevins, Victoria Road, Paisley PA2 9PT

Hon. Treasurer: **Mrs Jean Gillan,** 28 Walkerston Avenue, Largs KA30 8ER

DATES OF OPENING

Ardgowan, Inverkip	Sunday 9 February	2 – 5pm
Finlaystone, Langbank	Sunday 20 April	2 – 5pm
Renfrew Central Nursery	Sat & Sun 17/18 May	1 – 5pm
Stanely Crescent, Paisley	Sunday 25 May	2 - 5pm
Carruth Plant Sale, Bridge of Weir	Sunday 8 June	2 - 5pm
Lunderston, Ardgowan	Sunday 29 June	2 – 5pm
Duchal, Kilmacolm	Sunday 13 July	2 -5pm

ARDGOWAN, Inverkip ♿ (not advisable if wet)
(Sir Houston and Lady Shaw-Stewart)
Woodland walks carpeted with snowdrops. (Strong footwear advised). Tea in house.
Snowdrop stall, home baking and plant stall. Inverkip 1½ miles. Glasgow/Largs buses
in Inverkip.
Admission £1.00 Children under 10 free
SUNDAY 9th FEBRUARY 2 - 5 pm
40% to The National Trust for Scotland (Newhailes Appeal)

CARRUTH, Bridge of Weir ♿
(Mr & Mrs Charles MacLean)
PLANT SALE. Big selection of herbaceous, herbs and shrubs etc., in lovely country
setting. Beautiful trees and many different rhododendrons. Teas. Woodland walking.
Access from B786 Kilmacolm/Lochwinnoch road.
Admission £1.50
SUNDAY 8th JUNE 2 - 5pm
40% to Cancer Relief Macmillan Fund

DUCHAL, Kilmacolm &
(The Lord and Lady Maclay)
18th century walled garden, clipped hollies, azaleas. Old fashioned roses, shrubs and herbaceous borders with fruit orchards and vegetable garden. Lily pond. Loch and woodlands. . Plant and produce stall. Teas under cover. Kilmacolm 1 mile, B786. Greenock/Glasgow bus via Bridge of Weir; Knapps Loch stop is ¼ mile from garden. Admission £2.00 Children under 10 free
SUNDAY 13th JULY 2 - 5pm
40% to Strathcarron Hospice, Denny

FINLAYSTONE, Langbank &
(Mr & Mrs George G MacMillan)
Historic connection with John Knox and Robert Burns. Richly varied gardens with unusual plants overlooking the Clyde. A profusion of daffodils and early rhododendrons. Waterfalls & pond. Woodland walks with play and picnic areas. 'Eye-opener' centre with shop. Celtic and Dolly Mixture exhibitions. Ranger service. Plant stall. Teas in Celtic Tree.
Admission to House: £1.50 Children & OAPs £1.00. Langbank station 1 mile.
On A8 west of Langbank, 10 minutes by car west of Glasgow Airport.
Admission £2.00 Children & OAPs £1.20
SUNDAY 20th APRIL 2 - 5 pm
20% to Quarrier's Village 20% to Erskine Hospital

LUNDERSTON, Ardgowan, Inverkip &
(Dr J L Kinloch)
A six acre garden at sea level. Surrounding the House, shrubs, lawns, herbaceous borders and rose beds make a pleasant foreground to the view of the Firth of Clyde beyond. To one side of the house there is a kitchen garden which combines with a spacious greenhouse to provide fresh vegetables year round. The latest development lies beyond this and comprises extensive sweeps of grass bordered by impressive plantings of over two thousand roses. Plant stall. Teas. Enter Ardgowan at North Lodge and follow signs.
Admission £1.50 Children over 10 & OAPs £1.00
SUNDAY 29th JUNE 2 - 5pm
20% to Ardgowan Hospice 20% to Erskine Hospital

RENFREWSHIRE CENTRAL NURSERY, Hawkhead Road, Paisley &
(Renfrewshire Council)
Three-quarters of an acre under glass, intensively cropped, associated with Open Day demonstrations. Exhibitions of related crafts, countryside interpretation etc. Entertainments etc. Tea served in marquee. Plant stall. Gardeners' Roadshow celebrity panellists.
Admission £1.50 Children & OAPs 75p
25th Anniversary Opening.
SATURDAY & SUNDAY 17th & 18th MAY 1 - 5 pm
40% to Erskine Hospital

#STANELEY CRESCENT, Paisley

No. 17 Broomfield (Mr & Mrs J C Forrest)

Small landscaped garden overlooking Stanely Reservoir and ruined castle. Herbaceous border, lawns, fish and lily pond, azaleas and shrubs.

No. 25 (Mr & Mrs J B Wilson)

One acre woodland garden, specie and hybrid rhododendrons, camellias, magnolias, unusual shrubs and trees.

Teas at 22 Stanely Crescent (Mrs R Moffett). Plant stall.

Route: B775. Stanely Crescent is off Stanely Road, Paisley.

Admission £1.50 Children free when accompanied by adults.

SUNDAY 25th MAY 2 - 5pm

40% to Accord Hospice

ROSS, CROMARTY, SKYE & INVERNESS

District Organiser:	**Lady Lister-Kaye,** House of Aigas, Beauly IV4 7AD
Area Organisers:	**Mrs Robin Fremantle,** Fannyfield, Evanton IV16 9XA
Hon. Treasurer:	**Mr Kenneth Haselock,** 2 Tomich, Strathglass, Beauly IV4 7LZ

DATES OF OPENING

Abriachan Garden Nursery	February - November 9am - dusk
Attadale, Strathcarron	Easter-end October, not Suns. 10 - 5pm
Clan Donald, Isle of Skye	Daily all year
Coiltie, Divach, Drumnadrochit	Daily June - August 12 - 7pm
Dunvegan Castle, Isle of Skye	17 March - 31 October 10am-5.30pm
Glamaig, Braes, Isle of Skye	Daily Easter – mid-September
Leckmelm Shrubbery & Arboretum	Daily 1 April – 30 Sept 10am– 6pm
Sea View, Dundonnell	Tuesdays - Saturdays mid May to mid September or by appt.
Tournaig, Poolewe	By appointment

Inverewe, Poolewe	Saturday 26 April	9.30am – 9pm
Allangrange, Munlochy	Sunday 11 May	2 – 5.30pm
House of Gruinard, by Laide	Saturday 24 May	2 – 6pm
Tournaig, Poolewe	Wednesday 28 May	2 – 6pm
Attadale, Strathcarron	Saturday 31 May	2 – 6pm
Dundonnell, by Little Loch Broom	Thursday 5 June	2 – 5.30pm
Lochalsh Woodland Garden, Balmacara	Saturday 7 June	1 – 5.30pm
Allangrange, Munlochy	Sunday 8 June	2 – 5.30pm
Brahan, Dingwall	Sunday 8 June	2 – 5.30pm
Dundonnell, by Little Loch Broom	Wednesday 11 June	2 – 5.30pm
Achnashellach Station House	Fri & Sat 13/14 June	10am - 6pm
Kyllachy, Tomatin	Sunday 15 June	2 – 5.30pm
House of Gruinard, by Laide	Wednesday 25 June	2 – 6pm
Dundonnell, by Little Loch Broom	Thursday 3 July	2 – 5.30pm
Kilcoy Castle, Muir of Ord	Sunday 6 July	2 - 6pm
Dundonnell, by Little Loch Broom	Wednesday 9 July	2 – 5.30pm
Allangrange, Munlochy	Sunday 13 July	2 – 5.30pm
House of Aigas & Field Centre	Sat& Sun 26/27 July	10.30-5.30pm
Inverewe, Poolewe	Sunday 27 July	9.30am – 9pm
House of Aigas & Field Centre	Sat& Sun 2/3 August	10.30-5.30pm
Tournaig, Poolewe	Wednesday 6 August	2 – 6pm
House of Gruinard, by Laide	Saturday 9 August	2 – 6pm
House of Aigas & Field Centre	Sat& Sun 9/10 August	10.30-5.30pm
House of Aigas & Field Centre	Sat& Sun 16/17 August	10.30-5.30pm
Glencalvie, by Ardgay	Sunday 24 August	2 - 6pm

ABRIACHAN GARDEN NURSERY, Loch Ness Side
(Mr & Mrs Davidson)
An outstanding garden. Over 2 acres of exciting plantings, with winding paths through native woodlands. Seasonal highlights - hellebores, primulas, meconopsis, hardy geraniums and colour themed summer beds. Views over Loch Ness.
Admission by collecting box. Adults £1.00
FEBRUARY to NOVEMBER 9 am - dusk

ACHNASHELLACH STATION HOUSE
(Mr & Mrs P H Hainsworth)
A one acre garden started in 1975 by a plant enthusiast. Part old railway siding, part winding paths through a wild garden with a very wide range of plants and habitats. Fine mountain scenery and forest walks nearby. 9 miles east of Lochcarron. Cars take forest road (1 mile, courtesy Forestry Commission) 300 yards EAST of railway bridge over A890, or walk 400 yards from telephone box half mile WEST of railway bridge.
Admission £1.50
FRIDAY & SATURDAY 13th & 14th JUNE 10am - 6pm
40% to Association for the Protection of Rural Scotland

ALLANGRANGE, Munlochy, Black Isle &
(Major Allan Cameron)
A formal and a wild garden containing flowering shrubs, trees and plants, especially rhododendrons, shrub roses, meconopsis and primulas. Plants for sale. Exhibition of botanical paintings by Elizabeth Cameron. Teas in house. Inverness 5 miles. Signposted off A9.
Admission £1.50
SUNDAYS 11th MAY, 8th JUNE and 13th JULY 2 - 5.30 pm
40% to Highland Hospice

ATTADALE, Strathcarron
(Mr & Mrs Ewen Macpherson)
Ten acres of old rhododendrons, azaleas and unusual shrubs in woodland setting with views of Skye and the sea. Water gardens, woodland walk and sunken formal garden. On A890 between Strathcarron and South Strome.
Admission £1.50 Children & OAPs 75p
EASTER - end OCTOBER 10am - 5pm. Closed Sundays
Donation to Scotland's Gardens Scheme
SATURDAY 31st MAY 2 - 6pm   Teas in house. Plant stall.
40% to Highland Hospice

BRAHAN, Dingwall
(Mr & Mrs A Matheson)
Wild garden, dell with azaleas and rhododendrons. Arboretum with labelled trees and river walk. Home made teas in house. Maryburgh 1½ miles. Take road west from Maryburgh roundabout.
Admission £1.50 Children free
SUNDAY 8th JUNE 2 - 5.30 pm
40% to Highland Hospice

CLAN DONALD VISITOR CENTRE &

The "Garden of Skye" nestles in a sheltered corner of Skye's Sleat peninsula. The 40 acres of woodland garden are based around a 19th century collection of exotic trees. Much of the garden has been restored, displaying plants from around the world. New features include the ponds, rockery, herbaceous borders and terrace walk. Disabled facilities: toilet, wheelchair to borrow, companion of disabled person free admission. Visitor Centre open 24 March - 8 November.
Admission to Gardens £3.40   Children/concessions £2.20
Gardens OPEN ALL YEAR.
Donation to Scotland's Gardens Scheme

COILTIE, Divach, Drumnadrochit

(Gillian & David Nelson)
A wooded garden, an amalgamation of a Victorian flower garden abandoned 60 years ago and a walled field with a large moraine, which has been made over the past 15 years. Development work still in progress. Many trees, old and new, mixed shrub and herbaceous borders, roses, wall beds, rockery. No dogs please. Off A82 at Drumnadrochit. Take road signposted Divach uphill 2 miles. Beyond Divach Lodge 150m.
Admission £1.50 Children free
OPEN DAILY JUNE - AUGUST 12 - 7pm
20% to Scotland's Gardens Scheme   20% to Amnesty International

---

DUNDONNELL, by Little Loch Broom

(Mr Alan and Mr Neil Roger)
Garden includes a collection of bonsai, prehistoric yew tree and ancient holly about 1600 AD. Plants for sale. No dogs in garden, on leads in arboretum.
Dundonnell is on Little Loch Broom 31 miles west of Garve. Ullapool 24 miles.
Admission £1.50 Children 50p
**THURSDAY 5th JUNE, WEDNESDAY 11th JUNE,
THURSDAY 3rd JULY, WEDNESDAY 9th JULY 2 - 5.30 pm**
40% to the Army Benevolent Fund and the Police Dependants Fund

---

DUNVEGAN CASTLE, Isle of Skye

Dating from the 13th century and continuously inhabited by the Chiefs of MacLeod, this romantic fortress stronghold occupies a magnificent lochside setting. The gardens, originally laid out in the 18th century, have been extensively replanted and include lochside walks, woodlands and water gardens. Licensed restaurant. Two craft shops. clan exhibition. Seal colony. Loch boat trips. Admission to Castle and Garden inclusive £4.80, students, OAPs & parties £4.20, children £2.60. Dunvegan village 1mile, 23 miles west of Portree.
Admission to gardens: £3.50 Children £1.80
MONDAY 17th MARCH - FRIDAY 31st OCTOBER 10am - 5.30pm. Last entry 5pm
Donation to Scotland's Gardens Scheme

GLAMAIG, Braes, Portree, Isle of Skye

(Mr & Mrs R Townsend)
Two acres of mixed wild and informal garden with burn, waterfalls and extensive views of sea, islands and mountains. Large collection of unusual shrubs, rhododendrons, olearias etc. Primulas, herbaceous and rock garden. Some plants for sale. 7 miles from Portree at end of B883.
Admission £1.00 OAPs 50p
OPEN DAILY EASTER TO MID-SEPTEMBER
Donation to Scotland's Gardens Scheme

GLENCALVIE, by Ardgay &

(Glencalvie Estate)

Approx. 5 acres of lakeside, woodland and walled gardens. Newly planted (5 years) with continuing programme. Mainly shrubs, herbaceous and marsh plants. Riverside walk. Teas. Plant stall. From Ardgay follow signs to Croick, turn left at phone box and then third drive on left.

Admission £1.50 Children and OAPs £1.00

SUNDAY 24th AUGUST 2 - 6pm

40% to Carron Charitable Trust

The HOUSE of AIGAS and FIELD CENTRE, by Beauly

(Sir John and Lady Lister-Kaye)

Aigas has a woodland walk overlooking the Beauly River with a collection of named Victorian specimen trees now being restored and extended with a garden of rockeries, herbaceous borders and shrubberies. Tea in house. There is also a 1½ mile nature trail and rainbow trout fishing on Aigas Loch. Aigas Field Centre facilities are open to groups by appointment only: 01463 782443. Route: 4½ miles from Beauly on A831 Cannich/Glen Affric road.

Admission from £1.50

26th & 27th JULY, 2nd & 3rd AUGUST, 9th & 10th AUGUST, 16th & 17th AUGUST 10.30am - 5.30pm

Donation to Scotland's Gardens Scheme

HOUSE OF GRUINARD, by Laide

(The Hon Mrs Angus Maclay)

Wonderful west coast views. Herbaceous and shrub borders and water garden. Large variety of plants for sale. Sorry no teas.

Admission £1.50 Children under 16 free

SATURDAY 24th MAY, WEDNESDAY 25th JUNE, SATURDAY 9th AUGUST 2-6pm

40% to Highland Hospice

INVEREWE, Poolewe &

(The National Trust for Scotland)

Garden started in 1862 by Osgood Mackenzie. Eucalyptus, rhododendrons, and many more plants, some rare, from China, the Himalayas, Japan, Australasia, South Africa and Chile.   Visitor centre, shop and self-service restaurant.

Admission £4.50 Children & OAPs £3.00   Family Ticket £12.00

SATURDAY 26th APRIL and SUNDAY 27th JULY 9.30 - 9pm

40% to The Gardens Fund of the National Trust for Scotland

For further opening details see page 128

KILCOY CASTLE, Muir of Ord &

(Mr & Mrs Nick McAndrew)

16th century castle (not open) surrounded by extensive terraced lawns, walled garden with fine herbaceous and shrub borders, surrounding vegetable garden. Woodland areas with rhododendrons, azaleas and particularly fine mature trees and shrubs. Teas. Route: A9 to Tore roundabout, A832 signed Beauly and Muir of Ord. After 1½ miles, turn right at church signed Kilcoy, entrance is ½ mile on right.

Admission £1.50 Children 50p

SUNDAY 6th JULY 2 - 6pm

40% to Highland Hospice

KYLLACHY, Tomatin &

(The Rt Hon Lord & Lady Macpherson)

Rhododendrons (mainly white), azaleas, meconopsis, primulas, delphiniums, heather beds, herbaceous, alpines, iris. Water garden with stream and ponds. Walled vegetable garden. Plant stall. Tea. No dogs please. Cars free. A9 to Tomatin, turn off to Findhorn Bridge, turn west to Coignafearn. Kyllachy House one mile on right. Admission £1.50   Free car parking.

SUNDAY 15th JUNE 2 - 5.30 pm

40% to The Highland Hospice

LECKMELM SHRUBBERY & ARBORETUM, by Ullapool

(Mr & Mrs Peter Troughton)

The arboretum, planted in the 1870s, is full of splendid trees, specie rhododendrons, azaleas and shrubs. Warmed by the Gulf Stream, this tranquil woodland setting has an alpine garden and paths which lead down to the sea.

Parking in walled garden. Situated by the shore of Loch Broom 3 miles south of Ullapool on the A835 Inverness/Ullapool road.

Admission £1.50 Children under 16 free

OPEN DAILY 1st APRIL to 30th SEPTEMBER 10 am - 6 pm

20% to The Highland Hospice 20% to Scotland's Gardens Scheme

LOCHALSH WOODLAND GARDEN, Balmacara

(The National Trust for Scotland)

Passed to the Trust in 1953; main rhododendron planting by Euan Cox in early 60s. A garden in the making, with developing collections of Rhododendron, bamboo, ferns, Fuchsia and Hydrangea; mature beeches, oaks, pines and larches. Teas at Lochalsh House. On the shores of Loch Alsh, signposted off A87, 3m east of Kyle of Lochalsh. Admission £1.00 Children 50p

SATURDAY 7th JUNE 1 - 5.30 pm

40% to The Gardens Fund of The National Trust for Scotland

For other opening details see page 133

SEA VIEW GARDEN GALLERY, Durnamuck, Dundonnell &

(Simone & Ian Nelson)

Small, ½ acre cottage garden spectacularly positioned on the side of Little Loch Broom. The flourishing result of one woman's ongoing contest with virgin moor and the elements. Regret no dogs. Limited parking. Gallery - Ian Nelson watercolours . Plant stall. Refreshments available at the Dundonnell Hotel, 6 miles away. Signed off main A832 Gairloch/Dundonnell road at Badcaul for 1 mile.

Admission £1.00 Children free with adults

Tuesday - Saturday, mid MAY - mid SEPTEMBER

or by appointment. Tel: 01854 633317

20% to Dundonnell Area Community Events   20% to Cancer Relief Macmillan Fund

---

TOURNAIG, Poolewe & (partly)

(Lady Horlick)

Woodland, herbaceous and water garden. Plant stall. Tea in house. 1½ miles north of Inverewe Garden, Poolewe, on main road. Can be viewed at any time on request. Tel: 01445 781250 or 339.

Admission £1.50 Children under 12 free

WEDNESDAYS 28th MAY and 6th AUGUST 2 - 6 pm

20% to St John's Ambulance   20% to Crossroads Care Attendant Scheme

ROXBURGH

District Organiser: **Mrs M D Blacklock,** Stable House, Maxton,
St Boswells TD6 0EX

Area Organisers: **The Hon Moyra Campbell,** Scraesburgh,
Jedburgh TD8 6QR

Hon. Treasurer: **Mr J Mackie,** Bank of Scotland,
Newton St Boswells TD6 0PG

DATES OF OPENING

Floors Castle, Kelso .... Daily Easter to end September	10am – 4.30pm
October: Sundays & Wednesdays	10 am – 4pm
Mertoun, St Boswells .... Sunday 1 June	2 – 6pm
Benrig, Benrig Cottage, Mansfield House	
& Stable House, St Boswells .... Sunday 22 June	2 – 6pm
Corbet Tower, Morebattle .... Sunday 13 July	2 – 6pm
Monteviot, Jedburgh .... Sunday 20 July	2 – 5pm
Yetholm Village Gardens .... Sunday 3 August	2 – 6pm

BENRIG, St Boswells ♿
(Mr & Mrs Nigel Houldsworth)
Semi-walled garden with shrub roses and herbaceous plants. Magnificent views of the
River Tweed. Play area for toddlers. Cake stall.
JOINT OPENING WITH BENRIG COTTAGE, STABLE HOUSE and MANSEFIELD
HOUSE, SITUATED ON THE SAME ROAD. Plant stall and cream teas available at
Stable House. Parking at Benrig and Mansfield House for all four gardens. St Boswells:
2 minutes from A68 on the A699 to Kelso.
Admission £2.00 includes all gardens
SUNDAY 22nd JUNE 2 - 6pm
40% to Mertoun Kirk Heating Fund

BENRIG COTTAGE, St Boswells ♿
(Mrs J E Triscott)
A small garden incorporating roses, herbaceous plants and a small vegetable area. New
rose arbour. JOINT OPENING WITH BENRIG, MANSFIELD HOUSE and STABLE
HOUSE SITUATED ON THE SAME ROAD. Plant stall and cream teas available at
Stable House. Parking at Benrig and Mansfield House for all four gardens. St Boswells:
two minutes from A68 on the A699 to Kelso.
Admission £2.00, includes all gardens.
SUNDAY 22nd JUNE 2 - 6pm
40% to Mertoun Kirk Heating Fund

CORBET TOWER, Morebattle
(Mr & Mrs G H Waddell)

Scottish baronial house (1896) set in parkland in the foothills of the Cheviots. Garden includes formal parterre with old fashioned roses. Traditional walled garden with herbaceous borders, herbs and vegetables. Woodland and water garden. Teas. Plant and vegetable stall. From A68 Jedburgh road take A698, at Eckford B6401 to Morebattle, then road marked Hownam.

Admission £2.00 Children under 14 free

SUNDAY 13th JULY 2 - 6pm

40% to Jennifer Fund (Child Leukaemia Fund)

FLOORS CASTLE, Kelso &
(The Duke of Roxburghe)

Floors Castle is situated in beautiful Borders country, overlooking Kelso and the River Tweed. Extensive gardens, grounds and children's play area. Ample parking facilities. Garden Centre & Coffee Shop open daily 10.30 am - 5.30 pm; also Castle, grounds & restaurant. (Last admission to House 4 pm). Nearest town Kelso.

Open Daily EASTER to end SEPTEMBER 10am - 4.30pm

OCTOBER: Sundays & Wednesdays 10am - 4pm

Donation to Scotland's Gardens Scheme

MANSFIELD HOUSE, St Boswells
(Mr & Mrs D M Forsyth)

18th century manse sitting in one acre of established garden, containing mixed planting of trees, shrubs and clematis. Interesting traditional vegetable garden. JOINT OPENING WITH BENRIG, BENRIG COTTAGE and STABLE HOUSE SITUATED ON THE SAME ROAD. Plant stall and cream teas available at Stable House. Parking at Benrig and Mansfield House for all four gardens. St Boswells: 2 minutes from A68 on the A699 to Kelso.

Admission £2.00, includes all gardens.

SUNDAY 22nd JUNE 2 - 6pm

40% to Mertoun Kirk Heating Fund

MERTOUN, St Boswells &
(The Duke of Sutherland)

House built by Sir William Scott of Harden in 1703 to the design of Sir William Bruce. Remodelled 1956 by Ian G Lindsay, reducing house to original size. Shrubs, azaleas, redesigned herbaceous borders, ornamental pond, etc. View of the River Tweed. Home made teas. Jedburgh branch British Legion Pipe Band. Plant stall, raffle, cake stall, various other stalls, sideshows etc. St Boswells 2 miles. Driving south on the A68, turn left opposite The Buccleuch Arms Hotel, continue through village and on for about three-quarters of a mile over River Tweed to first Drive on the right.

Admission to garden £1.50 Children under 12 free

SUNDAY 1st JUNE 2 - 6 pm

40% to Maxton & Mertoun Kirks

MONTEVIOT, Jedburgh

Monteviot stands on a rise above the River Teviot overlooking the rolling Borders countryside. Features include a walled rose garden, shrub and herbaceous borders, water garden of islands linked by bridges, collection of rare trees in pinery.

Rose Day: Jedforest Instrumental Band. Children's activities. Cream teas in house. Stalls including cakes, plants and bottle tombola. Car park free. Dogs on lead. St Boswells 5 miles, Jedburgh 4 miles. Turn off A68 on to B6400 to Nisbet, north of Jedburgh. Entrance second turning on right.

Enquiries to (01835) 830380 9.30am-1pm Monday-Friday.

Admission £2.00 OAPs £1.00 Children under 14 free

SUNDAY 20th JULY (ROSE DAY) 2 - 5 pm

20% to St Mary's Church, Jedburgh
20% to Riding for the Disabled Association, Border Group

STABLE HOUSE, St Boswells &

(Lt Col & Mrs M D Blacklock)

House converted in 1982 and garden started in 1983. "A plant lovers garden. Here, in an informal design, unusual plants are combined with old fashioned roses, shrubs and herbaceous plants to give colour and interest all summer. All in half an acre; also a courtyard garden with tender climbers, small vegetable garden incorporated into mixed border and newly extended gold border."

JOINT OPENING WITH BENRIG, BENRIG COTTAGE AND MANSFIELD HOUSE SITUATED ON THE SAME ROAD.

Home made cream teas in Garden Room and Conservatory. Plant stall. Cake stall and raffle. Parking at Benrig and Mansfield House for all four gardens. St Boswells: two minutes from A68 on the A699 to Kelso.

Admission £2.00, includes all gardens.

SUNDAY 22nd JUNE 2 - 6pm

40% to Mertoun Kirk Heating Fund

YETHOLM VILLAGE GARDENS

2 Grafton Court & (Mr G Lee)   **Ivy House** & (Mr & Mrs Patterson)
Hill View (Mr & Mrs Dodds)   **4 Morebattle Road** (Mr & Mrs D White)
Copsewood (Mr & Mrs Fraser Nimmo)

Yetholm Village is situated at the foot of the Cheviot Hills with outstanding views. Each garden has its own endearing character and is filled with a variety of herbaceous shrubs, fruit trees and colourful bedding plants. Tickets will be sold on the Village Green where there will be a produce stall. Home baked teas. Ample parking.

Admission £1.50, includes all gardens.

SUNDAY 3rd AUGUST 2 - 6pm

40% to Childrens Hospice Association Scotland

STEWARTRY OF KIRKCUDBRIGHT

District Organiser:	**Mrs M R C Gillespie,** Danevale Park, Crossmichael, Castle Douglas DG7 2LP
Area Organisers:	**Miss P Bain,** Annick Bank, Hardgate, Castle Douglas DG7 3LD
	Mrs C Cathcart, Culraven, Borgue, Kirkcudbright DG6 4SG
	Mrs A Chandler, Auchenvin, Rockcliffe, Dumfries DG5 4QQ
	Mrs Jane Hannay, Kirklandhill, Kirkpatrick Durham, Castle Douglas DG7 3EZ
	Mrs W J McCulloch, Ardwall, Gatehouse of Fleet DG7 2EN
	Mrs C A Ramsay, Limits, St Johns, Dalry, Castle Douglas DG7 3SW
Hon. Treasurer:	**Mr W Little,** 54 St Andrew Street, Castle Douglas DG7 1EN

DATES OF OPENING

Cally Gardens, Gatehouse of Fleet .... Sats & Suns, Easter to first weekend in October 10am - 5.30pm
Corsock House, Castle Douglas .... By appointment

Danevale Park, Crossmichael................................	Sunday 2 March	2 - 5pm
Walton Park, Castle Douglas	Sunday 4 May	2 – 5pm
Barnhourie Mill, Colvend......................................	Sunday 18 May	2 – 5pm
Hensol, Mossdale..	Sunday 25 May	2 – 5pm
Corsock House, Castle Douglas	Sunday 1 June	2 – 5pm
High Trees, Gatehouse of Fleet	Sunday 15 June	2 - 5pm
Cally Gardens, Gatehouse of Fleet	Sunday 22 June	10am – 5.30pm
Southwick House, Dalbeattie	Sunday 29 June	2 – 5pm
	& afternoons 30 June - 5 July	
Argrennan House, Castle Douglas	Sunday 13 July	2 – 5pm
Threave School of Gardening	Sunday 3 August	9am-5.30pm
Cally Gardens, Gatehouse of Fleet	Sunday 10 August	10am – 5.30pm

ARGRENNAN HOUSE, Castle Douglas &
(Robert Reddaway & Tulane Kidd)
Georgian house set in beautiful parkland with specimen trees. A large walled garden with traditional herbaceous borders, shrub borders and rose garden. Water garden with box parterres and 1840 rockery. Woodland walks. Water garden, ponds and bog gardens. Plant stall. Teas served in old kitchen. House not open. Route: Castle Douglas 3½ miles. Kirkcudbright 3½ miles on A711.
Admission £2.00 Children 50p
SUNDAY 13th JULY 2 - 5 pm
40% to Crossroads Care Attendant Scheme (Stewartry branch)

111

BARNHOURIE MILL, Colvend ♿ (partly)

(Dr M R Paton)

Flowering shrubs and trees, dwarf conifers and an especially fine collection of rhododendron species. Tea in house £1. Cars free. Dalbeattie 5 miles. Route A710 from Dumfries.

Admission £2.00 Children free

SUNDAY 18th MAY 2 - 5pm

Also open by appointment. Tel: 01387 780269

40% to Scottish Wildlife Trust

CALLY GARDENS, Gatehouse of Fleet ♿

(Mr Michael Wickenden)

A specialist nursery in a fine 2.7 acre, 18th century walled garden with old vinery and bothy, all surrounded by the Cally Oak woods. Our collection of 3,000 varieties can be seen and many will be available pot-grown, especially rare herbaceous perennials. Forestry nature trails nearby. Route: From Dumfries take the Gatehouse turning off A75 and turn left, through the Cally Palace Hotel Gateway from where the gardens are well signposted. Voluntary admission charge.

Open every Saturday& Sunday from Easter to first weekend in October 10am- 5.30pm

SUNDAYS 22nd JUNE and 10th AUGUST 10 am - 5.30 pm

40% to Save the Children Fund

CORSOCK HOUSE, Castle Douglas

(Mr & Mrs M L Ingall)

Rhododendrons, woodland walks with temples , water gardens and loch. David Bryce turretted "Scottish Baronial" house in background. Teas by Corsock WRI. Cars free. Dumfries 14 miles, Castle Douglas 10 miles, Corsock ½ mile on A712.

Admission £2.00 Children 50p

SUNDAY 1st JUNE 2 - 5 pm

Also open by appointment: Tel. 01644 440250

40% to Gardeners' Royal Benevolent Society

DANEVALE PARK, Crossmichael

(Mrs M R C Gillespie)

Open for snowdrops. Woodland walks. Tea in house. Route: A713. Crossmichael 1 mile, Castle Douglas 3 miles. Admission £1.50

SUNDAY 2nd MARCH 2 - 5pm

40% to Crossmichael Village Hall

HENSOL, Mossdale, Castle Douglas ♿

(Lady Henderson)

An early 19th century granite house designed by Lugar. Established garden surrounding house. Alpines, shrubs, water garden and new woodland garden. River walks. Plant stall. Cars free. Tea in house. Route: A762, 3 miles north of Laurieston.

Admission £2.00 Children 50p

SUNDAY 25th MAY 2 - 5 pm

40% to John Paul Jones Birthplace Museum

HIGH TREES, Gatehouse of Fleet
(Dr & Mrs R G Law)
Two acres of mainly wooded hillside garden featuring the National Collection of Eucalypts. More than 600 labelled trees, shrubs and herbaceous plants including many azaleas and rhododendrons. Also several unusual plants from the southern hemisphere, particularly Tasmania, and a number of natural rockeries with a wide variety of alpines. Teas. Plant stall. No dogs please. Route: A75 to Gatehouse of Fleet. Parking in Community Centre with free minibus service - 3 minutes - to and from garden.
Admission £2.00 Children 50p OAPs £1.00
SUNDAY 15th JUNE 2 - 5pm
40% to Lions, Gatehouse branch

SOUTHWICK HOUSE, Dalbeattie ♿ (formal garden only)
(Mrs C H Thomas)
Formal garden with lily ponds and herbaceous borders, shrubs, vegetables, fruit and greenhouse. Water garden with boating pond, lawns and fine trees, through which flows the Southwick burn. Tea & biscuits, ice cream and soft drinks. On A710, near Caulkerbush. Dalbeattie 7 miles, Dumfries 17 miles.
Admission £2.00 Children 50p
SUNDAY 29th JUNE 2 - 5 pm, also 30th JUNE - 5th JULY with honesty box
40% to Childline Scotland

THREAVE SCHOOL OF GARDENING, Castle Douglas ♿
(The National Trust for Scotland)
Baronial house by Peddie & Kinnear. 60 acres of garden. Ornamental, fruit, vegetable and glasshouses. House not open. Plant stall. Route: A75, one mile west of Castle Douglas.
Admission £3.70 Children & OAPs £2.50
SUNDAY 3rd AUGUST 9.30am - 5.30pm
40% to The Gardens Fund of The National Trust for Scotland
For other opening details see page 132

WALTON PARK, Castle Douglas ♿
(Mr Jeremy Brown)
Walled garden, gentian border. Flowering shrubs, rhododendrons and azaleas. Cars free. Tea in house. Plant stall. Route: B794, 3½ miles from A75.
Admission £2.00
SUNDAY 4th MAY 2 - 5 pm
40% to Carnsalloch Cheshire Home

TWEEDDALE

District Organiser: **Mrs John Kennedy,** Hazlieburn, West Linton EH46 7AS

Area Organisers: **Mrs D Balfour-Scott,** Langlawhill, Broughton,
                          Lanarkshire ML12 6HL

                       Mrs R K Brown, Runic Cross, Waverley Road,
                          Innerleithen EH44 6QH

                       Mrs H B Marshall, Baddinsgill, West Linton, EH46 7HL

Hon. Treasurer: **Mr K St C Cunningham,** Hallmanor, Peebles EH45 9JN

DATES OF OPENING

Kailzie Gardens, Peebles .... Daily 22 March – 18 October   11 – 5.30pm
Winter daylight hours, gardens only

Barns, Kirkton Manor .... Sunday 20 April   2 - 5.30pm
Dawyck Botanic Garden .... Sunday 11 May   10am – 6pm
Hallmanor, Kirkton Manor .... Sunday 8 June   2 – 6pm
Stobo Water Garden, Stobo .... Sunday 15 June   2 – 6pm
Cringletie House Hotel, Eddleston .... Sat & Sun 28/29 June   2 – 5pm
Portmore, Eddleston .... Sunday 27 July   2 – 5pm
West Linton Village Gardens .... Sunday 3 August   2 - 6pm

---

 # BARNS, Kirkton Manor ♿ (partially)
(Lady Elizabeth & Mr David Benson)
The property is the setting for John Buchan's "John Burnet of Barns". Late 16th century peel tower and 1773 house with stable block set in an extensive area of snowdrops and daffodils on the Tweed. Fledgeling arboretum. Teas. Route: Turn off A72 to Kirkton Manor for 1½ miles; turn right into 1 mile drive. Parking near house.
Admission £1.50 Children free
SUNDAY 20th APRIL 2 - 5.30pm
40% to Manor & Lyne Churches

CRINGLETIE HOUSE HOTEL, Eddleston ♿
(Mr & Mrs S L Maguire)
House by David Bryce. Former home of Wolfe Murray family, set in 28 acres of woodlands, including walled garden which includes fruit trees, vegetables etc. Herbaceous borders. Tea 3.30 - 4.30 pm. Cars free. Peebles 2½ miles. Donation box. Bus: No.62 Edinburgh/Peebles. Hotel signposted from A703 Edinburgh/Peebles. SGS signs.
SATURDAY 28th JUNE 2 - 5 pm
40% to St Columba's Hospice
SUNDAY 29th JUNE 2 - 5 pm
40% to the Royal Blind Asylum

DAWYCK BOTANIC GARDEN, Stobo   ᴕ (limited access)
(Specialist Garden of the Royal Botanic Garden, Edinburgh)
Arboretum of rare trees, rhododendrons and other shrubs. Terraces and stonework constructed by Italian landscape gardeners in 1820. Conservatory shop with plant sales, coffees and teas. Guide dogs only. Route: 8 miles south west of Peebles on B712.
Admission £2.00 Concessions £1.50 Children 50p Families £4.50
SUNDAY 11th MAY 10 am - 6 pm
40% to Royal Botanic Garden, Edinburgh
For other opening details see page 139

HALLMANOR, Kirkton Manor, Peebles
(Mr & Mrs K St C Cunningham)
Rhododendrons and azaleas, primulas, wooded grounds with loch and salmon ladder. Set in one of the most beautiful valleys in the Borders. Teas. Plant stall. Peebles 6 miles. Off A72 Peebles/Glasgow road. Follow SGS signs.
Admission £1.50 Children free
SUNDAY 8th JUNE 2 - 6 pm
40% to Manor & Lyne Churches

KAILZIE GARDENS, Peebles ᴕ
(Lady Buchan-Hepburn)
Semi-formal walled garden with rose garden, herbaceous borders and old fashioned roses. Greenhouses. Woodland and burnside walks among massed spring bulbs and, later, rhododendrons and azaleas. The gardens, set among fine old trees, lie in the beautiful Tweed valley with views across to the Border hills. Free car park. Picnic area. Children's play corner. Home made teas and lunches in licensed restaurant. Art Gallery. Shop. Plant stalls. Stocked trout pond. Parties by arrangement.
Admission: Summer £2.00, children 5-14 50p Winter £1.00, children 50p
OPEN ALL YEAR ROUND Summer: 22nd March - 18th October 11am - 5.30pm.
Winter: during daylight hours, the gardens only.
Special Snowdrop Days as advertised locally.
Donation to Scotland's Gardens Scheme

PORTMORE, Eddleston
(Mr & Mrs D H L Reid)
Herbaceous borders. Herb garden. Ornamental vegetable garden. Greenhouse with Victorian grotto. Newly planted shrub rose garden and parterre. Cream teas. Dogs on lead please. Edinburgh to Peebles bus No.62.
Admission £2.00
SUNDAY 27th JULY 2 - 5 pm
40% to Crossroads Care Attendant Scheme

STOBO WATER GARDEN, Stobo, Peebles
(Mr Hugh Seymour & Mr Charles Seymour)
Water garden, lakes, azaleas and rhododendrons. Woodland walks. Cars free. Cream teas in village hall. Peebles 7 miles, signposted on B712 Lyne/Broughton road.
Admission £1.50 Children free
SUNDAY 15th JUNE 2 - 6 pm
20% to Stobo Kirk   20% to Marie Curie Cancer Care

WEST LINTON VILLAGE GARDENS ♿ (partially)
A number of gardens, small and large, varying from an extensive selection of original stone troughs, to a well established plantsman's garden. Also traditional summer bedding and a small walled garden. Route: A701 or A702 and follow signs. Tickets & maps available at car park or Graham Institute (Teas & Plant Stall) in centre of village. Admission £2.00 includes all gardens. Children free
SUNDAY 3rd AUGUST 2 - 6pm
20% to Crossroads Care Attendant Scheme   20% to Earl Haig Fund

WIGTOWN

District Organiser:	**Mrs Francis Brewis,** Ardwell House, Stranraer DG9 9LY
Area Organisers:	**Mrs V WolseleyBrinton,** Chlenry, Castle Kennedy, Stranraer DG9 8SL
	Mrs Andrew Gladstone, Craichlaw, Kirkcowan, Newton Stewart DG8 0DQ
Hon. Treasurer:	**Mr G S Fleming,** Bank of Scotland, 64 George Street, Stranraer DG9 7JN

DATES OF OPENING

Ardwell House Gardens, Ardwell .... Daily 28 March- 30 September   10am–5pm
Castle Kennedy & Lochinch Gardens,
      Stranraer .... Daily 28 March–30 Sept.   10am-5pm
Whitehills, Newton Stewart .... 1 April – 31 October by appointment

Logan, Port Logan...................................... Sunday 25 May   10am - 6pm
Logan Botanic Garden, Port Logan........................ Sunday 25 May   10am – 6pm
Monreith House Garden, Port William .... Sunday 25 May   10am - 5pm
Whitehills Garden & Nursery, Newton Stewart.... Sunday 1 June   2 - 5pm
Bargaly House, Palnure .... Sunday 15 June   2 – 5pm

ARDWELL HOUSE GARDENS, Ardwell, Stranraer
(Mrs Faith Brewis & Mr Francis Brewis)
Daffodils, spring flowers, rhododendrons, flowering shrubs, coloured foliage and rock plants. Moist garden at smaller pond and a walk round larger ponds, with views over Luce Bay. Plants for sale and self-pick fruit in season. Collecting box. House not open. Dogs welcome on leads. Picnic site on shore. Teas available in Ardwell village. Stranraer 10 miles. Route A76 towards Mull of Galloway.
Admission £1.50 Children & OAPs 50p
DAILY 28th MARCH to 30th SEPTEMBER 10 am - 5 pm
Donation to Scotland's Gardens Scheme

BARGALY HOUSE, Palnure, Newton Stewart &

(Mr Jonathan Bradburn)

Unusual trees and shrubs in extensive borders, rock and water garden, walled garden with large herbaceous border. Woodland and river walks. Refreshments available. Palnure 2 miles, A75. Bus stop, Palnure.

Admission £1.50 Children 50p

SUNDAY 15th JUNE 2 - 5 pm

Donation to Scotland's Gardens Scheme

CASTLE KENNEDY & LOCHINCH GARDENS, Stranraer &

(The Earl & Countess of Stair)

The gardens are laid out on a peninsula betwen two lochs and extend to 75 acres from the ruined Castle Kennedy to Lochinch Castle. They are world famous for rhododendrons, azaleas, magnolias and embothriums and contain specimens from Hooker and other expeditions. Choice of peaceful walks. Plant centre. Gift shop with refreshments. Admission charged. 20% discount for parties over 30 people. Cars and disabled free. Stranraer 5 miles on A75. For further information telephone 01776-702024.

DAILY 28th MARCH - 30th SEPTEMBER 10 am - 5 pm

Donation to Scotland's Gardens Scheme

LOGAN, Port Logan, by Stranraer   &

(Mr & Mrs M Coburn)

Queen Anne house, 1701. Rare exotic tropical plants and shrubs. Fine specie and hybrid rhododendrons. Route: 14 miles south of Stranraer on A716, 2½ miles from Ardwell village. JOINT OPENING WITH LOGAN BOTANIC GARDEN.

Admission £2.00 includes both gardens Concessions £1.50 Children 50p Families £4.50

SUNDAY 25th MAY 10 am - 6 pm

40% to Port Logan Hall Fund

LOGAN BOTANIC GARDEN, Port Logan, by Stranraer &

(Specialist Garden of the Royal Botanic Garden Edinburgh)

One of the most exotic gardens in Britain. Magnificent tree ferns and cabbage palms grow within a walled garden together with a rich array of southern hemisphere plants. Licensed Salad Bar and Shop with gifts, crafts and plant sales; open 10am to 6pm. Guide dogs only. Route: 10m south of Stranraer on A716, then 2½ miles from Ardwell village. JOINT OPENING WITH LOGAN.

Admission £2.00 includes both gardens Concessions £1.50 Children 50p Families £4.50

SUNDAY 25th MAY 10 am - 6 pm

40% to Royal Botanic Garden Edinburgh

For other opening details see page 139

MONREITH HOUSE GARDEN, Port William

(Sir Michael Maxwell Bt)

Once famous garden created by Sir Herbert Maxwell, one of the great pioneers of Scottish gardening. It has been neglected for over 50 years, but restoration began last year and is continuing. Interesting trees and shrubs. Teas. 2m from Port William off B7021 Port William/Whithorn.

Admission £2.00 Children & OAPs £1.00 includes entry to House.

SUNDAY 25th MAY 10am - 5pm

40% to Monreith Trust

WHITEHILLS GARDEN & NURSERY, Newton Stewart ♿
(Mr & Mrs C A Weston)
Informal garden set among mature trees. Large collection of unusual trees and
flowering shrubs. Rhododendrons and azaleas (many grown from seeds collected by
owners in China and Nepal) grow amidst sheltered woodland. Ample parking.
Newton Stewart 1 mile. Wood of Cree road ¼ m north of Minnigaff Church (signposted
to RSPB reserve). Dogs on lead please.
Admission £1.50 Accompanied children under 14 and disabled in wheelchairs free.
Concessions £1.00 Family £5.00
SUNDAY 1st JUNE 10am - 5pm Open by appointment 1 April - 31 October: 01671 402049
40% to Friends of Newton Stewart Hospital

Overlooking the Clyde
10 min west of Glasgow Airport on A8
west of Langbank

Finlaystone

Eye-Opener Centre with
* Shop
* Clan MacMillan Centre
* Celtic Art Exhibition
* "Dolly Mixture" Doll Collection

Gardens with richly varied and unusual plants and pond
Mansion House with historic connection with Robert Burns and John Knox
Woodland walks with play and picnic areas

OPEN THROUGHOUT THE YEAR – 10.30 - 5.00
Historic house with Victorian Kitchen open Sundays April - August
Tours at 2pm, 3pm and 4pm or by appointment
Lunch and tea in the **"Celtic Tree"** in the Walled Garden
(Open April - September)
Group bookings welcome Tel. 01475 540285 (House) or 01475 540505 (Ranger)
Finlaystone, Langbank, Renfrewshire PA14 6TJ

Manderston

Nr Duns, Berwickshire

Home of the Lord and Lady Palmer

"THE SWANSONG OF THE GREAT CLASSICAL HOUSE"

Outside, 56 acres of immaculate gardens with a lake by which visitors can walk. Inside, a house on which no expense was spared. Here one can see superb, sumptuous staterooms decorated in the Adam manner and the only silver staircase in the world. The amazingly sophisticated "below stairs" domestic quarters give an intriguing insight into life in a large house at the turn of the century. A Biscuit Tin Museum was opened in 1984.

There are not only the extensive formal and woodland gardens but princely stables and an extravagant marble dairy.

Cream teas are served for visitors on Open Days. There is also a shop selling souvenirs and home-made goods.

Open: 2.00-5.30p.m. Thursdays and Sundays, May 18th to September 28th.

Also Bank Holiday Mondays, May 26th and August 25th, 2.30p.m.-5.30p.m.

Parties any time of year by appointment. Telephone: Duns (01361) 883450.

GARDENS OF SCOTLAND
1998

Hot off the press !!
Order your copy now and it will be posted
to you without delay.

To: SCOTLAND'S GARDENS SCHEME
31 CASTLE TERRACE, EDINBURGH EH1 2EL

Please send _____ copy / copies of "Gardens of Scotland 1998" at £3.75 each, inclusive of postage, *as soon as it is available.* I enclose a cheque / postal order payable to Scotland's Gardens Scheme.

Name ....

Address ....

....

.... Post Code ....

GARDENS IN TRUST

THE NATIONAL TRUST FOR SCOTLAND is custodian to some of Scotland's finest gardens, from the world-famous Inverewe and Crathes Castle Gardens to the undeservedly less visited such as Inveresk Lodge and Malleny Gardens near Edinburgh and Leith Hall near Huntly.

The Trust's work in conserving this heritage of gardens is greatly enhanced by the enjoyment of them by several hundred thousand visitors each year. Visitors, whether members of the Trust or not, contribute financially to the upkeep of our gardens.

Although Trust gardens are open most days of the year, we also give active support to Scotland's Gardens Scheme, opening many of our gardens on its behalf on special days during the year. A selection of National Trust for Scotland gardens is described in the following pages.

The hunt for the Brodie daffodils

Between 1899 and 1942, Major Ian Brodie, the 24th laird of Brodie, meticulously raised tens of thousands of daffodil seedlings at Brodie Castle, from which he selected only some 440 as being worthy of naming.

His rigorous standards and his contacts with other daffodil enthusiasts – several of whom used his stock for their own breeding programmes – have helped to fashion the way these popular garden plants have evolved.

Sadly, only a handful of Brodie's seedlings remain commercially available today. Worse still, by the time The National Trust for Scotland acquired Brodie Castle in 1978, only a fraction of these plants could be identified with any certainty from within the grounds there. However, most of Brodie's plants were commercially available earlier this century, and daffodils, as bulbous plants, are relatively persistent... so there is a good chance more remain in cultivation, if we can find them.

Can you help? If you have a named or indexed collection of daffodils, or know that you have Brodie daffodils (such as 'Banchory', 'Forfar', 'Lovat Scout', or 'Perth'), please contact the NTS Gardens Department at 5 Charlotte Square, Edinburgh EH2 4DU.

Major Ian Brodie among his daffodils

Arduaine Garden

Argyll & Bute. On A816, 20 miles from Oban and Lochgilphead

Branklyn Garden

A85, Dundee Road, Perth

THIS ATTRACTIVE plantsman's garden at Arduaine occupies a spectacular site overlooking Loch Melfort. It has a superb collection of rhododendrons and specimen trees. Some of these are of remarkable size.

The garden was first created by J A Campbell between 1900 and 1930. In 1971, brothers Harry and Edmund Wright bought the garden from the Campbell family and began restoration and improvement. In 1992 they presented the garden to the Trust.

Open all year, daily 9.30 a.m.—sunset. Admission: adult £2.30, child/concession £1.50, adult party £1.80, child/school party £1 (family £6.10).

Free entry for The National Trust for Scotland Members.

ON A PERTH HILLSIDE, looking southward over the Tay, Branklyn has been described as "the finest two acres of private garden in the country". Between 1922 and 1966 Mr & Mrs John Renton made an outstanding collection of plants, particularly of alpines, and Sino-Himalayan species. These were laid out, mainly by Dorothy Renton, with a good eye for complementary plant association. This legacy lives on: unusual plants, densely and attractively planted.

Open 1 March to 31 October, daily 9.30 — sunset. Admission: adult £2.30, child/concession £1.50, adult party £1.80, child/school party £1 (family £6.10).

Free entry for The National Trust for Scotland Members.

♛ The National Trust for Scotland

Brodick Castle, Garden and Country Park

**Isle of Arran. Ferry from Ardrossan
(and Kintyre in summer)**

BRODICK CASTLE and its gardens came into the care of the Trust in 1958 following the death of the Duchess of Montrose, whose home it was. She created a woodland garden, considered one of the finest rhododendron gardens in Europe. Plants from the Himalayas, Burma and China flourish in the gentle west coast climate and give a continuous display of colour from January to August. The formal garden is 250 years old and has recently been restored as a Victorian garden. A country park was established in 1980 through an agreement between Cunninghame District Council and the Trust.

Special nature trail for disabled. Wheelchairs available. Braille sheets.

Open: Castle, 1 April (or Good Friday if earlier) to 31 October, daily 11.30 – 5 (last admission 4.30). Reception Centre and shop (dates as castle), 10 – 5; restaurant 11– 5. Garden and Country Park, all year, daily 9.30 – sunset.

GOATFELL: open all year.

Admission: Castle and garden, adult £4.50, child/concession £3, adult party £3.60, child/school party £1, family £12. Garden only, adult £2.30, child/concession £1.50, adult party £1.80, child/school party £1. Car park free. Ferry from Ardrossan (55 minutes) to Brodick. Connecting bus, pier to castle (2 miles). Ferry enquiries to Caledonian MacBrayne: tel. Gourock (01475) 650100.

Free entry for The National Trust for Scotland Members.

☗ The National Trust for Scotland

Crathes Castle and Garden

Aberdeenshire
On A93, 3 miles east of Banchory and 15 miles west of Aberdeen

THE CASTLE AND ITS GARDENS are situated near Banchory, in a delightful part of Royal Deeside. Formerly Crathes was the home of Sir James and Lady Burnett of Leys, whose lifelong interests found expression in the gardens and in one of the best plant collections to be found in Britain. Sir James experimented with trees and shrubs, many from the Hillier Nurseries, while Lady Sybil was one of the first disciples of Gertrude Jekyll. From an earlier age come specimen yews, said to date from 1702. Wheelchair access to garden and grounds, trail for disabled, shop, exhibitions, adventure playground, restaurant and toilets for disabled visitors. Wheelchairs available.

Open: Castle, Visitor Centre, shop and licensed restaurant . 1 April (or Good Friday if earlier) to 31 October, daily 11 – 5.30 (last admission to castle 4.45); plant sales, same dates except weekends only in Oct. Other times by appointment only. Garden and grounds, all year, daily 9.30 – sunset. To help you enjoy your visit and for safety reasons, admission to the castle is by a timed ticket arrangement. Grounds may be closed at short notice on very busy days due to the limited capacity for car parking.

Admission: Castle only, adult £1.80, child/ concession £1.20, combined ticket (castle, garden and grounds), adult £4.50, child/ concession £3, adult party £3.60, child/school party £1, family £12. Grounds only/walled garden only, adult £1.80, child/concession £1.20. Grounds and walled garden, adult £3.60, child/concession £2.40.

Enquiries and all bookings: tel: Crathes (01330) 844525.

Free entry for The National Trust for Scotland Members.

☙ The National Trust for Scotland
Culzean Castle, Garden and Country Park

South Ayrshire

A719, 4 miles south-west of Maybole and 12 miles south of Ayr

CULZEAN CASTLE AND COUNTRY PARK is the Trust's most visited garden property and one of the major tourist attractions in Scotland.

The range of interests and activities at Culzean make it a perfect day out for the family. The Fountain Garden lies in front of Robert Adam's magnificent Castle, with terraces and herbaceous borders reflecting its Georgian elegance.

Scotland's first Country Park, consisting of 563 acres, contains a wealth of interest from shoreline through Deer Park, Swan Pond to mature parklands, gardens, woodland walks and adventure playground. A conservatory has been restored to its former glory as an orangery. Ranger/Naturalists located at the Visitor Centre provide excellent services for visitors including many guided walks. An environmental education service and interpretation programme are based on the Country Park.

The Visitor Centre facilities include a shop, licensed self-service restaurant, introductory exhibition to Culzean, auditorium and information. For disabled—lift in castle, toilets, wheelchairs, induction loop for hard of hearing.

Open: Castle, Visitor Centre, licensed restaurant and shops, 1 April (or Good Friday if earlier) to 31 October, daily 10.30 – 5.30 (last admission 5). Other times by appointment. Country Park, all year, daily 9.30 – sunset. Admission: Castle only, adult £4, child/concession £2.70, family £10.70; Country Park only, adult £3, child/concession £2; adult party £2.50, school coach £20, family £8. Combined ticket, Castle and Country Park, adult £6, child/concession £4, adult party £4.80, family £16.

Enquiries and all party bookings: tel. Kirkoswald (01655) 760269.

Free entry for The National Trust for Scotland members.

☙ The National Trust for Scotland

Culross Palace Garden

Fife
Off A985, 12 m west of Forth Road Bridge

I
n 1994 the Trust reopened Culross Palace and Garden following three years of restoration. The Palace, built between 1597 and 1611, was not a royal palace but the home of Sir George Bruce, a wealthy merchant and pioneer entrepreneur.

A model seventeenth-century garden created by the Trust shows a selection of the plants which might have been available to Sir George Bruce to support the needs of his household. These include a range of vegetables, culinary and medicinal herbs, soft fruit, ornamental shrubs and herbaceous perennials. Terraced and on a steep slope, the garden is laid out in a series of raised beds. Willow hurdle fences, crude rustic plant-supports and crushed-shell paths add to the period effect.

Open: Palace, 1 April (or Good Friday if earlier) to 30 September, daily 11-5 (last admission 4). Town House & Study, same dates, 1.30– 5 and weekends in Oct., 11 – 5. Groups at other times by appt. Tearoom (in Bessie Bar Hall), dates as Town House, 10.30 – 4.30. Admission: combined ticket to Palace, Study & Town House, adult £4, child/concession £2.70, adult party £3.20, child/school party £1 (family £10.70). **Free entry for The National Trust for Scotland Members.**

Falkland Palace Garden

Fife
A912, 11 miles north of Kirkcaldy

T
HE ROYAL GARDEN at Falkland Palace in Fife, which the Stuart Kings and Queens of Scotland knew, was restored after the war by the late Keeper, Major Michael Crichton Stuart, M.C., M.A., to a design by Percy Cane. Trees and shrubs and herbaceous borders give a long-lasting display from spring-flowering cherries to the rich autumn colouring of the maples. The greenhouse provides a colourful show during the greater part of the year. Ramp into garden for wheelchairs.

Open: Palace & garden, 1 April (or Good Friday if earlier) to 31 October, Monday – Saturday 11 – 5.30, Sunday 1.30 – 5.30 (last admission to palace 4.30, to garden 5). Groups at other times by appointment. Town Hall, by appointment only.

Admission: palace and garden, adult £4.50, child/concession £3, adult party £3.60, child/ school party £1, (family £12). Garden only, adult £2.30, child/concession £1.50, adult party £1.80, child/school party £1. Scots Guards and members of the Scots Guards Association (wearing the Association's badge) admitted free.

Free entry for The National Trust for Scotland Members.

♕ The National Trust for Scotland

Hill of Tarvit
Fife. Off A916
2¹/₂ miles south of Cupar

Inveresk Lodge Garden
East Lothian. A6124 south of
Musselburgh, 6 miles east
of Edinburgh

THIS MANSION HOUSE and garden were remodelled by Sir Robert Lorimer in 1906 for Mr F. B. Sharp. Although the garden has developed and consequently changed, much of the original Lorimer design remains. The garden is still being developed with the object of creating greater interest and colour during the year. Bequeathed in 1949 by Miss E. C. Sharp.

Open: House, Good Friday to Easter Monday and 1 May to 30 September, daily 1.30 – 5.30, weekends in October, 1.30 – 5.30 (last admission 4.45). Tearoom, same dates, but opens 12.30. Garden & Grounds, all year, daily 9.30–sunset.

Admission: House and garden, adult £3.50, child/concession £2.30, adult party £2.80, child/ school party £1, (family £9.30). Garden & grounds only, £1 (honesty box).

Free entry for The National Trust for Scotland Members.

INVERESK, on the southern fringes of Musselburgh, is one of the most unspoiled villages of the Lothians. The 17th century Lodge (which is not open to the public) is the oldest building in the village. The garden has been almost completely remodelled since the Trust was presented with the property, and an endowment, by Mrs Helen E. Brunton in 1959. This reconstruction is rather similar to the garden as it was in 1851. This is a happy coincidence, for the old plan was found after the present layout was completed. There are good examples of shrubs, trees and other plants for smaller gardens, many having the RHS Award of Garden Merit.

Open: 1 April to 30 September, Monday – Friday 10 – 4.30, Saturday/Sunday 2 – 5, 1 October to 31 March, Monday – Friday 10 – 4.30, Sunday 2– 5.

No dogs in garden please. Cars may be parked only by garden wall.

Admission: £1 (honesty box).

Free entry for The National Trust for Scotland Members.

♥ The National Trust for Scotland

Inverewe Garden

Highland

On A832, by Poolewe, 6 miles north-east of Gairloch

THIS MAGNIFICENT HIGHLAND GARDEN, near Poolewe, is in an impressive setting of mountains, moorland and sea-loch and attracts over 130,000 visitors a year. When it was founded in 1862 by Osgood Mackenzie, only a dwarf willow grew where plants from many lands now flourish in a profusion as impressive as it is unexpected. Planned as a wild garden it includes Australian tree ferns, exotic plants from China, and a magnificent *Magnolia campbellii*. Given into the care of the Trust in 1952 by Mrs Mairi T. Sawyer, together with an endowment. Disabled access to greenhouse and 50 per cent of paths. Wheelchairs available. Toilets.

Open: garden, 15 March to 31 October, daily 9.30–9, 1 November to 14 March daily 9.30– 5. Visitor Centre and shop, 15 March to 31 October, daily 9.30 – 5.30. Licensed restaurant, same dates, daily 10 – 5. Guided garden walks, 15 March to 30 September, Monday to Friday at 1.30.

No dogs in garden. No shaded car parking.

Admission: Adult £4.50, child/concession £3, adult/cruise party £3.60, child/school party £1 (family £12).

Free entry for The National Trust for Scotland Members.

♥ The National Trust for Scotland

Kellie Castle Garden

Fife

On B9171, 3 miles north north-west of Pittenweem

THE PRESENT GARDEN is largely as restored by Sir Robert Lorimer and his sister, Louise, in the early 20th century after Professor James Lorimer, Sir Robert's father, had restored and made his home at Kellie Castle. A delightful model of a late Victorian garden with box-edged paths, rose arches, many period roses, herbaceous plants, soft and tree fruits and a collection of interesting old-fashioned vegetables. Video programme. Tearoom. Wheelchair access to garden. Induction loop for the hard of hearing.

Open: Castle, Good Friday to Easter Monday and 1 May to 30 September, daily 1.30 – 5.30; weekends in October 1.30 – 5.30 (last admission 4.45). Garden and grounds, all year, daily 9.30 – sunset.

Admission: Castle and garden, adult £3.50, child/concession £2.30, adult party £2.80, child/school party £1 (family £9.30). Garden and grounds only £1 (honesty box).

Free entry for The National Trust for Scotland Members

Leith Hall Garden

**Aberdeenshire. On B9002,
1 mile west of Kennethmont and
34 miles north-west of Aberdeen**

THIS ATTRACTIVE old country house at Kennethmont, Aberdeenshire, the earliest part of which dates from 1650, was the home of the Leith and Leith-Hay families for more than three centuries. The west garden was made by Mr and The Hon. Mrs Charles Leith-Hay around the beginning of the present century and has a spectacular herbaceous border. The rock garden was enhanced by the Scottish Rock Garden Club in celebration of their 150th anniversary. The Leith-Hays also improved the eastern vegetable garden: the moon gate is notable, as are the striking views over the surrounding countryside. The property was given to the Trust by The Hon. Mrs Leith-Hay in 1945. Toilet for disabled. Picnic area.

Open: house and tearoom, Good Friday to Easter Monday and 1 May to 30 September, daily 1.30 – 5.30; weekends in October, 1.30 – 5.30 (last admission 4.45). Garden and grounds, all year, daily 9.30 – sunset.

Admission: adult £4, child/concession £2.70, adult party £3.20, child/school party £1 (family £10.70). Garden and grounds only, adult £1.80, child/concession £1.20, adult party £1.50, child/school party £1.

Free entry for The National Trust for Scotland Members

Priorwood Garden

**Borders
A6091, in Melrose**

THIS SMALL FORMAL GARDEN specialising in flowers for drying is situated in the middle of Melrose, adjacent to Melrose Abbey. Features include herbaceous borders and beds of annual flowers suitable for drying. A wide range of information and drying aids, together with dried flowers from the garden, are on sale. Orchard walk containing unusual fruit. The property was purchased by the Trust in 1974.

Open: 1 April (or Good Friday if earlier) to 30 September, Monday – Saturday 10 – 5.30, Sunday 1.30 – 5.30. 1 October to 24 December, Monday – Saturday 10 – 4, Sunday 1.30 – 4.

NTS Shop in Abbey Street, 9 January to 31 March, Monday – Saturday 12 – 4; 1 April to 24 December, Monday – Saturday 10 – 5.30, Sunday 1.30 – 5.30. Closed 31 October to 7 November for stocktaking.

Admission: £1 (honesty box).

Best seen June to October.

Free entry for The National Trust for Scotland Members.

The National Trust for Scotland

Pitmedden Garden

**Aberdeenshire. On A920, 1 mile west of
Pitmedden village and 14 miles north of Aberdeen**

AT PITMEDDEN, near Udny, The National Trust for Scotland has re-created a model parterre garden on the site of the 17th-century "Great Garden" originally laid out by Sir Alexander Seton, the first baronet of Pitmedden. Three of the parterre sections derive from designs once used at Holyrood in Edinburgh and the fourth is a tribute to the Setons, using their family crest. Fountains and sundials make excellent centrepieces to the garden, spectacularly filled in summer with 40,000 annual flowers. The Museum of Farming Life has now grown to become one of the best exhibitions on farming life in the north-east. Extensive herbaceous borders, fruit trees and herb garden. Facilities for the disabled. Garden room. Tearoom. Visitor Centre. Shop. Guided tours available.

Open: Garden, Visitor Centre, museum, tearoom, grounds & other facilities, 1 May to 30 September, daily 10–5.30, last admission 5.

Admission: Garden and museum, adult £3.50, child/concession £2.30, adult party £2.80, child/ school party £1 (family £9.30). Garden and grounds only, £1 (honesty box).

Free entry for The National Trust for Scotland Members.

☙ The National Trust for Scotland

Threave Garden

Dumfries and Galloway
Off A75, 1 mile west of Castle Douglas

THIS VICTORIAN MANSION HOUSE near Castle Douglas, Dumfries and Galloway Region, with policies, woodland and gardens extending in all to 1,490 acres, was presented to the Trust with an endowment in 1947 by the late Major A. F. Gordon of Threave. In 1960 the house was adapted for use for a school of horticulture, giving particular emphasis to practical training within the 60-acre gardens. A diverse amenity garden with an outstanding plant collection has been developed since then.

Open: Estate & garden, all year, daily 9.30 – sunset. Walled garden and glasshouses, all year, daily 9.30 – 5. Visitor Centre, exhibition and shop, 1 April (or Good Friday if earlier) to 31 October, daily 9.30 – 5.30. Restaurant 10–5.

Admission: adult £3.70, child/concession £2.50, adult party £3, child/school party £1 (family £9.90).

Free entry for The National Trust for Scotland Members.

HEAD GARDENERS' MEETING

The National Trust for Scotland arranges an annual meeting of Head Gardeners from Trust and privately owned gardens. The objects are to enable gardeners to maintain contact with others in their profession and to keep up to date with recent technical developments, and to allow visits to be made to local gardens or nurseries of interest. Meetings are normally based in a hall of residence.

Owners or staff from gardens which are open under Scotland's Gardens Scheme are welcome to apply for one of the limited places available. Please ask for further details from the Gardens Department, The National Trust for Scotland, 5 Charlotte Square, Edinburgh EH2 4DU (telephone (0131) 226 5922).

☙ The National Trust for Scotland
OTHER TRUST GARDEN PROPERTIES
(Free entry for The National Trust for Scotland Members)

BRODIE CASTLE, MORAY
A garden being restored to include a selection of the Brodie collection of daffodils and other varieties. Interesting mature trees and avenue. Open: castle, 1 Apr (or Good Friday if earlier) to 30 Sep, Mon-Sat 11-5.30, Sun 1.30-5.30; weekends in Oct, Sat 11-5.30, Sun 1.30-5.30 (last admission 4.30). Other times by appointment. Grounds, all year, daily 9.30 – sunset.
Admission: adult £4, child/concession £2.70; adult party £3.20, child/ school party £1, family £10.70. Grounds only (outwith summer season's published opening times): £1 (honesty box).

BROUGHTON HOUSE, KIRKCUDBRIGHT, DUMFRIES AND GALLOWAY
A charming one-acre garden created by the artist E.A. Hornel between 1901 and 1933, which includes a 'Japanese-style' garden influenced by his many visits to the Far East. The garden includes many fine shrubs and herbaceous perennials. Open: house and garden, 1 Apr (or Good Friday if earlier) to 31 Oct, daily 1-5.30 (last admission 4.45)
Admission: adult £2.30, child/concession £1.50; adult party £1.80, child/school party £1, family £6.10.

CASTLE FRASER, ABERDEENSHIRE
A landscaped park with good trees and a walled garden which has been redesigned in a formal manner. Open: castle, Good Friday to Easter Monday, 1 May to 30 Jun and 1 to 30 Sep, daily 1.30-5.30; 1 July to 31 Aug, daily 11-5.30; 1.30-5.30 (last admission 4.45). Tearoom, dates as castle, but opens 12.15 in Sep. Garden, all year, daily 9.30-6; grounds, all year, daily 9.30-sunset.
Admission: castle, garden and grounds, adult £4, child/concession £2.70; adult party £3.20, child/school party £1, family £10.70. Garden and grounds only, adult £1.80, child/concession £1.20; adult party £1.50, child/school party £1.

DRUM CASTLE, ABERDEENSHIRE
Interesting parkland containing a fascinating collection of trees, 100 acre Wood of Drum, Arboretum and Garden of Historic Roses. Open: Castle, Good Friday to Easter Monday and 1 May to 30 Sep, daily 1.30-5.30; weekends in Oct, 1.30-5.30 (last admission 4.45). Garden, same dates, daily 10-6. Grounds, all year, daily 9.30–sunset.
Admission: castle, garden and grounds, adult £4, child/concession £2.70; adult party £3.20, child/school party £1, family £10.70. Garden and grounds only, adult £1.80, child/concession £1.20; adult party £1.50, child/school party £1.

GREENBANK GARDEN, CLARKSTON, GLASGOW
A Gardening Advice Centre offering a series of regular guided walks. Extensive plant collection set in thematic displays and demonstration gardens including special garden for the disabled. Open: all year, daily 9.30-sunset, except 25/26 Dec and 1/2 Jan. Shop and tearoom, 1 Apr (or Good Friday if earlier) to 31 Oct, daily 11-5. 1 Nov to 31 Mar, Sat & Sun 2–4. House open 1 Apr to 31 Oct, Sundays only, and during special events (subject to functions in progress). No dogs in garden please.
Admission: adult £2.80, child/concession £1.90; adult party £2.30, child/school party £1, family £7.50.

THE HILL HOUSE, HELENSBURGH
The garden at The Hill House complements the finest example of the domestic architecture of Charles Rennie Mackintosh and is being restored to represent the designs of Walter Blackie with features by Mackintosh.Open: 1 Apr (or Good Friday if earlier) to 31 Oct, daily 1.30-5.30 (last admission 5); tearoom, 1.30-4.30. **Increasing visitor numbers are placing great strain on the structure of The Hill House, which was designed for domestic purposes. Access may be restricted at peak times and at the discretion of the Property Manager.** Admission: adult £4.50, child/concession £3; adult party £3.60, child/school party £1, family £12.

HOUSE OF DUN, MONTROSE, ANGUS
Restoration of the gardens is based largely on designs originally conceived by Lady Augusta FitzClarence using typical plants of the 1840s. Upgrading of the woodlands and their former footpaths is also being carried out. Open: house and shop, Good Friday to Easter Monday and 1 May to 30 Sep, daily 1.30-5.30; weekends in Oct, 1.30-5.30 (last admission 5). Restaurant, same dates, but opens 12.30. Garden and grounds, all year, daily 9.30-sunset.
Admission: house, garden and £3.50, child/concession £2.30; adult party £2.80, child/school party £1, family £9.30. Garden and grounds only, £1 (honesty box).

MALLENY GARDEN, BALERNO, EDINBURGH
This 17th-century house (not open to the public) has a delightfully personal garden with many interesting plants and features, and a particularly good collection of shrub roses. National Bonsai Collection for Scotland. Open: garden, 1 Apr to 31 Oct, daily 9.30-7; 1 Nov to 31 Mar, daily 9.30-4. House not open. Admission: £1 (honesty box).

LOCHALSH WOODLAND GARDEN, BALMACARA, HIGHLAND
The woodland garden around Lochalsh House was begun in 1979 following successful experimental rhododendron plantings by E.H.M. Cox in the 1950s; these are complemented by collections of hardy ferns, hydrangeas, fuchsias and *Arundinaria* bamboos. Open: estate, all year, woodland garden daily 9 – sunset. Admission: woodland garden £1 (honesty box).

☸ The National Trust for Scotland
26 Beautiful Gardens to Visit

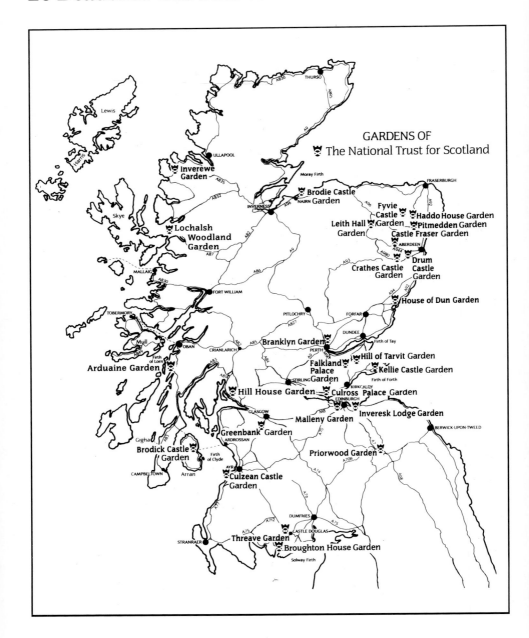

GARDENS OF
☸ The National Trust for Scotland

Inverewe Garden

Brodie Castle Garden

Fyvie Castle

Haddo House Garden

Leith Hall Garden

Pitmedden Garden

Lochalsh Woodland Garden

Castle Fraser Garden

Drum Castle Garden

Crathes Castle Garden

House of Dun Garden

Branklyn Garden

Hill of Tarvit Garden

Falkland Palace Garden

Kellie Castle Garden

Arduaine Garden

Hill House Garden

Culross Palace Garden

Inveresk Lodge Garden

Malleny Garden

Greenbank Garden

Priorwood Garden

Brodick Castle Garden

Culzean Castle Garden

Threave Garden

Broughton House Garden

☙ The National Trust for Scotland
Scotland's leading conservation organisation

THE NATIONAL TRUST FOR SCOTLAND belongs to you—to the people who love Scotland—and opens its properties for the enjoyment of all. That's why the brooding magnificence of Glencoe, the soaring mountains of Kintail, the peaceful beaches of Iona and so many great gardens are there for all to see and enjoy, protected for posterity.

At Inverewe Garden, palm trees grow on the same latitude as Labrador. From Brodick Castle Garden the rhododendrons win prizes at flower shows on both sides of the Atlantic. And at The NTS School of Practical Gardening, Threave, we train the head gardeners of the future.

But maintaining properties costs money. At Culzean Castle, Robert Adam's masterpiece overlooking the Clyde, the stonework is eroded by time and needs continual restoration. Repairs to the viaduct, and many other buildings on the estate now

in progress, will take a team of stonemasons several years to complete. And the contents of our properties require as much attention and painstaking care as the exteriors. The Trust has its own bookbinding, metalwork, picture-framing and furniture restoration workshops.

Gardens need replanting, curtains frayed with age require to be repaired, and paths on mountains worn by feet need re-seeding. We repair leaky roofs, antiquated plumbing and rusting suits of armour. The list is endless. Each year it costs the Trust almost £14m to carry out this work, quite apart from any new projects we may wish to undertake. That's why we need your help.

If you love the countryside and have a special place in your heart for Scotland, you can help its preservation by joining The National Trust for Scotland. On the next page you will find another six good reasons for joining.

☙ The National Trust for Scotland

Benefits of Membership

WE DON'T ASK FOR MUCH: we believe that we give so much in return. For example the cost of a single membership for a 12-month period is £25.00 and a whole family can join for £42.00—less than an average family night out.

In exchange we give you:

1 Free admission to over 100 properties in Scotland, plus over 300 properties of The National Trust, a completely separate organisation, in England, Wales and Northern Ireland.

2 Our quarterly colour magazine, *Heritage Scotland*, with lists of events, winter activities and a host of opportunities for you to enjoy.

3 For those who would like to do a little more, details of how to join one of our Members' support groups.

4 Priority booking for our holiday cottages, and an opportunity to book for our adventure base camps for groups, St Kilda work parties, and Thistle Camps for young people. Details of our Cruises.

5 Our annual illustrated *Guide to Over 100 Properties* listing opening times and facilities.

6 Facilities at our properties for all the family—grandparents, parents and children—including shops with our specially designed range of goods—and tearooms when you need to take the weight off your feet.

The National Trust for Scotland is a charity, independent of Government, supported by 230,000 members

JOIN Scotland's leading conservation organisation

Membership Enrolment Form

Rates valid until 31 October 1997

☐ Member: £25.00 or more per annum.
☐ Family: £42.00 or more per annum. Two adults at one address (and any of their children, under 18).
☐ Life: £500.00 or more (includes cardholder's children under 18).
☐ 25 & under: *£10.00 or more per annum (23 yrs and under).   Date of birth __/__/__
Concessions: Over 60s may join at a discount of 33.3% off full rates:
Member £17.00* ☐   Joint Members £28.00* ☐   Life Member £335.00 ☐
*Concessionary annual rates are not available to overseas residents due to administration costs.

I enclose remittance for/please charge my Credit Card £_____ Expiry date __/__

Visa/Access/American
Express/JCB/Mastercard/Switch No:

Please print

Mr/Mrs/Miss/Ms Surname_____Initials_____

Address:_____

_____

_____Postcode:_____

FOR NTS USE ONLY		
MEMBERSHIP NO.		
TYPE		SOURCE
		214
DAY	MONTH	YEAR
Amount received		
£		

Please send to: Membership Services, The National Trust for Scotland, 5 Charlotte Square, Edinburgh EH2 4DU

THE FINER SIDE OF SCOTTISH LIFE

An affordable, comfortable, year round extra room designed and crafted in Scotland, using timber or UPVC. A Cairn Conservatory will extend and complement your home for years to come.

- Built in Scotland to suit the Scottish climate
- Widely varied 'Standard' designs and a 'Made to Measure' range, individually designed to suit awkward situations
- We offer Full build service – all trades from Planning to Completion

- Free Survey, Design Drawings and Quotation
- 'Maintenance Free' roofs in toughened glass or polycarbonate
- High security multi-point locking systems
- 10 year Insurance Backed Guarantee
- Wide selection of Cane furniture and blinds available

Cairn Conservatories and a range of Cane Furniture are available for personal inspection at our Showroom at:

Cairn Conservatories Ltd.
Killearn Mill, Killearn, by Glasgow G63 9LQ

or Telephone for Full Colour Brochure.
Tel: 01360 550922   Fax: 01360 550616
Showroom open 7 days a week
Opening Hours – Weekdays: 9.00am – 5.00pm.
Week-ends: 1.00pm – 4.00pm

137

ROYAL BOTANIC GARDEN EDINBURGH

The Royal Botanic Garden Edinburgh displays its living collections in four outstanding gardens – Edinburgh, Younger, Logan and Dawyck.

ROYAL BOTANIC GARDEN EDINBURGH
One of the World's Great Gardens

Discover the wonders of the plant kingdom in Scotland's premier garden. Over 70 acres of beautifully landscaped grounds include the world-famous Rock Garden, the Pringle Chinese Collection and a magnificent Arboretum.

The amazing Glasshouse Experience, featuring Britain's tallest Palm House, leads you on a trail of discovery through Asia, Africa, the Mediterranean and the Southern Hemisphere.

The Botanics Shop for plants, books, stationery, gifts, children's goods and much, much more.

The licensed Terrace Cafe provides morning coffee, afternoon tea or lunch. Dill's Snack Bar provides light refreshments.

Full programme of events and exhibitions.

Facilities available for functions and events hire.

Admission free. Donations welcome. Open daily (except 25 December and 1 January): November–February, 10am– 4pm; March–April, 10am–6pm; May–August, 10am–8pm; September–October, 10am–6pm.

Royal Botanic Garden Edinburgh, 20A Inverleith Row, Edinburgh EH3 5LR.
One mile north of city centre, off A902. Telephone 0131 552 7171. Fax 0131 552 0382.

FRIENDS *of the*
Royal Botanic Garden Edinburgh

Joining the Friends enables you to support the vital work of Scotland's Botanic Garden. Through the Friends you can enjoy a close relationship with this great institution and learn more about the fascinating world of gardening, plants and science. You can participate in Friends events where you meet like-minded people: lectures, guided walks, garden visits, plant auctions of special Garden plants and plant sales. Membership entitles you to free entry to RBG Kew.

Your membership can make a positive difference – it costs as a little as £15 a year (family members £20 a year)

JOIN THE FRIENDS AND SUPPORT THE GARDEN

Come to the Friends Plant Sale on Sunday 8 June, 2.30pm, at the Garden Nursery, Inverleith Avenue South. All welcome.

Write to The Friends Office, Royal Botanic Garden Edinburgh, 20A Inverleith Row, Edinburgh EH3 5LR. Telephone 0131 552 5339

YOUNGER BOTANIC GARDEN BENMORE – A BOTANICAL PARADISE

Enter the magnificent avenue of Giant Redwoods and follow a variety of trails through the formal garden and hillside woodlands to a viewpoint with its spectacular outlook over the Holy Loch and the Eachaig Valley.

World famous collection of rhododendrons and conifers.

The Botanics Shop has a range of interesting gifts, souvenirs, books and some plants seen in the Garden. The licensed James Duncan Cafe offers delicious coffee, lunch or light snacks. Shop and Cafe open to non-Garden visitors. Cafe available for hire.

SPECIAL SCOTLAND'S GARDEN SCHEME OPENING 27 APRIL 1997.
FREE GUIDED TOURS WITH NORMAL DAY ADMISSION.

Younger Botanic Garden Benmore, Dunoon, Argyll PA23 8QU.
On A815, 7 miles north of Dunoon.
Telephone 01369 706261. Fax 01369 706369.

LOGAN BOTANIC GARDEN – SCOTLAND'S MOST EXOTIC GARDEN

Take a trip to the south west of Scotland and experience the southern hemisphere! Logan's exceptionally mild climate allows a colourful array of tender exotics to thrive out-of-doors – tree ferns, cabbage palms, unusual shrubs, climbers and tender perennials.

New for 1997 – the Discovery Centre, packed with interactive exhibits and displays that introduce you to the Garden and the fascinating world of plants.

The Botanics Shop stocks a range of appealing local crafts, gifts and cards not to mention a selection of Logan's best loved plants. Award winning licensed Salad Bar for coffee, lunch and light snacks.

SPECIAL SCOTLAND'S GARDEN SCHEME OPENING 25 MAY 1997

Logan Botanic Garden, Port Logan, Wigtownshire DG9 9ND.
On B7065, 14 miles south of Stranraer.
Telephone 01776 860231. Fax 01776 860333.

DAWYCK BOTANIC GARDEN – RENOWNED HISTORIC ARBORETUM

Follow the landscaped walks through the arboretum and discover Dawyck's secrets. Amongst mature specimen trees – some over 40 metres tall – are a variety of flowering trees, shrubs and herbaceous plants. Explore the world's first Cryptogamic Sanctuary and Reserve for 'non-flowering' plants.

A bright conservatory, where you can relax with coffee or tea and cakes, houses The Botanics Shop with carefully selected plants, books, local crafts and stationery. Among the plants on sale will be the Dawyck Beech, Brewer's Spruce and a wide range of species rhododendrons.

SPECIAL SCOTLAND'S GARDEN SCHEME OPENING 11 MAY 1997.

Dawyck Botanic Garden, Stobo, Peeblesshire EH45 9JU.
On B712, 8 miles southwest of Peebles.
Telephone 01721 760254. Fax 01721 760214.

Specialist Gardens of the Royal Botanic Garden Edinburgh Open: 15 March to 31 October (Dawyck 22 October), 10am to 6pm (and at other times by arrangement). Admission: adult £2.00, concession £1.50, child 50p, family £4.50, season tickets with special benefits available.

CLAN DONALD

V I S I T O R   C E N T R E

The 'Garden of Skye' nestles in a sheltered corner of Skye's Sleat peninsula. The 40 acres of woodland garden are based around a 19th century collection of exotic trees. Much of the garden has been restored, displaying plants from around the world. New features include the ponds, rockery, herbaceous borders and terrace walk

'MUSEUM OF THE ISLES'   COUNTRYSIDE RANGER SERVICE   GIFT SHOPS   RESTAURANT   LUXURY SELF CATERING COTTAGES

CLAN DONALD VISITOR CENTRE
Telephone: 01471 844305 Fax: 01471 844275

Visit GLEN GRANT DISTILLERY & GARDEN

Discover the mysteries of a very
special malt whisky, and enjoy a stroll up the
enchanting garden, carefully restored to
its original Victorian glory.

Opening Times
Mid March to end of May and October
Monday - Saturday 10am - 4pm Sunday 11.30am - 4pm
June to September
Monday - Saturday 10am - 5pm   Sunday 11.30am - 5pm

Under 18s admitted free.
Children under the age of 8 are NOT ADMITTED to production areas.

Glen Grant Distillery & Garden, Rothes, Aberlour AB38 7BS
Telephone: 01542 78 3318   Fax: 01542 78 3304

MARIE CURIE CANCER CARE 'FLOWERING OF SCOTLAND' APPEAL 1998

Could you join in our celebrations?

Marie Curie Cancer Care is looking for Garden owners in Scotland prepared to open their Garden in 1998 as a one-off to benefit Marie Curie Cancer Care during our Appeal year. This could be as an extra opening day or as part of your usual garden opening, perhaps during a 'yellow' flowering season - Daffodils for example - or at any other convenient time.

Marie Curie Cancer Care

In 1998 Marie Curie Cancer Care is celebrating its 50th Anniversary which in Scotland has particular significance as the first Marie Curie Hospice was at Hill of Tarvit in Fife. The 'Flowering of Scotland' Appeal aims to raise £4,000,000 before December 1998 for the two Marie Curie Centres in Scotland at Hunters Hill in Glasgow and at Fairmile in Edinburgh and also for the Marie Curie Nursing Service in Scotland.

By the end of 1998 one daffodil bulb will have been planted for each of our five million Scots forming huge 'Fields of Hope' throughout Scotland. 2,500,000 daffodil bulbs have already been planted for Marie Curie Cancer Care over the past five years and we plan to plant another 2,500,000 daffodil bulbs during 1998. Each bulb will be sponsored for £1.00 by the public with the names of all donors printed in a Commemorative Book of Hope, to be housed in the National Library of Scotland.

For further details please contact:

**Sarah Grotrian,
Marie Curie Cancer Care, 29 Albany Street, Edinburgh EH1 3QN.
Telephone 0131-478 7050   Facsimile 0131-478 7051**

Charity Registered No. 207994

THE GARDEN
Tuesday 8th July 1997

Entries are now invited for our annual auction of garden furniture and statuary, paintings, books, antique tools and ephemera.

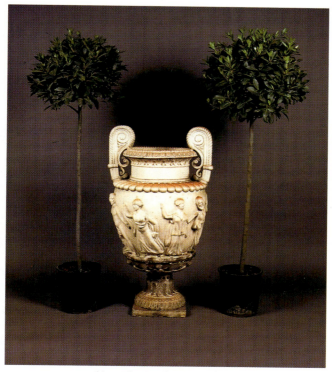

*Sold in The Garden Sale, July '96
for £3,200*

Enquiries: Campbell Armour on 0141 221 8377

65 George Street, Edinburgh EH2 2JL. 0131 225 2266.
207 Bath Street, Glasgow G2 4HD. 0141 221 8377.

A UNIQUE CELEBRATION FOR THE THIRD MILLENNIUM
SCOTLAND'S
GARDEN
The originality of Scotland's Garden
will win world acclaim for Scotland
Scotland is already famous for its scenic, sporting, cultural and culinary attractions.
Scotland's Garden, a world-class horticultural and environmental centre, which will be an entertaining fun experience for all.
Location: two hundred acre park near Stirling
Opening: 2000
Further information: Simon Beck (01786 452074)
http://www.gardenweb.com

Torosay Castle & Gardens
Craignure
Isle of Mull PA65 6AY

Telephone: 01680 812421 Fax: 01680 812470

Torosay is a beautiful and welcoming Victorian family home surrounded by 12 acres of spectacular gardens which offers an exciting contrast between formal terraces, impressive statue walk, woodland and water gardens

Open: April - mid October daily 10.30am - 5.30pm
Gardens only, open all year – daylight hours

Admission: Adult £4.50 Child £1.50 Concessions £3.50 Family £10.00
Tearoom. Craft/souvenir shop. Free car and coach parking. Groups welcome.

DRUMMOND CASTLE GARDENS, PERTHSHIRE

Scotland's most important formal gardens, among the finest in Europe. The upper terraces offer stunning views and overlook a magnificent parterre celebrating the saltire, family heraldry and the famous multiplex sundial by John Milne, Master Mason to Charles I.

OPEN EASTER WEEKEND, THEN DAILY MAY 1ST TO OCTOBER 31ST 2PM - 6PM (LAST ENTRY 5PM)

Coach party and wheelchair access by arrangement.

Tel: 01764 681257   Fax: 01764 681550

Entrance 2 miles south of Crieff on A822

Featured recently in United Artists' "Rob Roy"

HOLIDAYS

Brightwater Holidays are Scotland's specialist Garden Tour Operators. Our fully inclusive itineraries combine the famous and grand gardens with small and private gardens - most tours also visit specialist nurseries. Travel by comfortable coach from a variety of local pick-up points throughout Scotland and the UK. Tours for 1997 include:

Inverewe & the private gardens of Wester Ross

Highland & Island Gardens - the gardens of Argyll

In an English Country Garden including Sissinghurst

Gardens of the Far North including the Castle of Mey

Tresco & the Gardens of Cornwall

The Chelsea Flower Show

Monet's Garden & the Gardens of Normandy

Dutch Bulbfields Cruise

Austrian Alpine Gardens

If you have your own group and are looking for a tailor-made itinerary we are happy to work to suit your interests and budget. For brochure and full details Contact:-

Brightwater Holidays

Eden Park House, Cupar, Fife KY15 4HS

Tel: 01334 657155 Fax: 01334 657144

**ABTOT No. 5001 - A fully bonded tour operator
for your financial protection**

ABTOT
No. 5001

146

THE MURREL GARDENS

Aberdour, Fife KY3 0RN (off B9157)

The Garden was replanted with rare and unusual plants in 1982 and is now reaching maturity.

It is open every Wednesday from 10am to 5pm from April to October. It will also be open on 13th and 14th September in aid of Scotland's Gardens Scheme.

The Garden is not suitable for wheelchairs.

Admission charge £2

No dogs please.

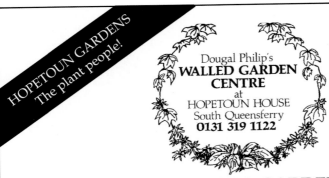

THE BUCCLEUCH ESTATES
invite you to visit

BOWHILL HOUSE & COUNTRY PARK, Nr Selkirk (Scottish Borders)

18/19th century house in beautiful countryside. Outstanding art collection, fine French furniture and relics of Duke of Monmouth, Sir Walter Scott and Queen Victoria.

Exciting Adventure Woodland Play Area. Audio-visual Visitor Centre. Nature Trails. Picnic Areas. Restored Victorian Kitchen. Tea Room. Gift Shop.

OPEN 1997

House	1-31 July daily 1-4.30
Country Park	26 April to 25 August incl. daily except Fridays 12-5. Open on Fridays during July with House.

Telephone No.   Selkirk (01750) 22204

Off A708—St. Mary's Loch-Moffat Road 3 miles west of Selkirk. Edinburgh 42 miles, Glasgow 75 miles, Berwick 43 miles, Newcastle 80 miles, Carlisle 56 miles.

Bowhill House

DRUMLANRIG CASTLE GARDENS & COUNTRY PARK Nr Thornhill, Dumfriesshire (South-west Scotland)

Castle built 1679-91 on a 15th century Douglas stronghold. Set in parkland ringed by wild hills. French furniture. Paintings by Rembrandt, Holbein and Leonardo. Bonnie Prince Charlie relics. Gift shop. Tea Room. Exciting Adventure Woodland Play Area. Picnic Sites. Nature Trails. Birds of Prey Centre. Visitors Centre. Craft Centre.

OPEN 1997

Castle and	Saturday 3 May to Monday 31 August incl.
Country Park	Daily 11 - 5, last entry 4.15pm. Castle closed Thursdays.
Telephone:	(01848) 330248 - Castle (01848) 331555 - Country Park

Off A76, 4 miles north of Thornhill. Glasgow 56 miles, Dumfries 18 miles, Edinburgh 56 miles, Carlisle 51 miles.

Drumlanrig Castle

BOUGHTON HOUSE, Nr Kettering (Northamptonshire)

Northamptonshire home of the Dukes of Buccleuch and their Montagu ancestors since 1528. Important art collection, French and English Furniture and Tapestries. "A vision of Louis XIV's Versailles transported to England".

Exciting Adventure Woodland Play Area. Nature Trail. Tea Room. Gift Shop. Garden Centre.

OPEN 1997

Grounds	1 May-15 September incl. 1-5 daily, except Fridays.
House and Grounds	1 August-1 September, 2-5 daily. (Grounds open 1 p.m.).

Telephone No.   Kettering (01536) 515731.

Off A43, 3 miles north of Kettering. Northampton 17 miles, Cambridge 45 miles, Coventry 44 miles, Peterborough 32 miles, Leicester 26 miles, London 50 minutes by train.

Boughton House

DALKEITH PARK, Nr Edinburgh (Lothian Region) Dalkeith Palace not open to public

Nature Trails. Woodland and riverside walks in the extensive grounds of Dalkeith Palace. Tunnel Walk. Adam Bridge. Fascinating Architecture. Exciting Adventure Woodland Play Area. Picnic Area. Barbecue facilities. Information Centre. Scottish farm animals. Ranger service. Come to our new Cafeteria/Shop in our restored Adam stable.

OPEN 1997

Grounds	26 March-29 October incl. 10 am-6 pm daily & weekends in winter.

Telephone Nos.   0131-663 5684, 665 3277 or 654 1666

Access from east end of Dalkeith High Street.

Off A68, 3 miles from Edinburgh City Bound

Dalkeith Palace from the Nature Trail

Parties welcome at all these estates (Special terms and extended opening times for pre-booked parties over 20).
All the houses have special facilities for wheelchair visitors.

149

All is well
in the garden
if you bank with
Adam & Company

The Complete Private Banking Service.

Flora Macdonald and Mark Hedderwick
22 Charlotte Square, Edinburgh EH2 4DF. Tel: 0131-225 8484

Don Bremner and Christopher Smith
238 West George Street, Glasgow G2 4QY. Tel: 0141-226 4848

ROYAL HORTICULTURAL SOCIETY MEMBERSHIP PRUNED BY £5.

As a special introductory offer to readers of Gardens of Scotland we're offering £5 off the cost of joining the Royal Horticultural Society. For just £27 you can get the best gardening advice and inspiration there is. (Normal price £32 - £25 plus £7 one-off enrolment fee). Every month you receive your own copy of The Garden magazine, packed with news, articles, problem pages and offers for members. Membership also gives you free visits to 25 gardens, as well as privileged tickets to the world's top flower shows, including the first ever Scotland's National Gardening Show in May. All you have to do is fill in the coupon and send it with a cheque for £27 to The Membership Department, The Royal Horticultural Society, PO Box 313, London SW1P 2PE. Tel: 0171-821 3000. This offer ends on October 31 1997. Clip the coupon below and cut the cost of membership.

———————— **GARDENS OF SCOTLAND SPECIAL RHS MEMBERSHIP OFFER.** ————————

I would like to join the RHS. Please make your cheque for £27 payable to The Royal Horticultural Society and send to: The Royal Horticultural Society, Membership Department, PO Box 313, London SW1P 2PE (Complete in capital letters).

Title _____ *Initials* _____ *Surname* _____

Address _____

Postcode _____ *Daytime Tel No.* _____

153

VISIT THE ST ANDREWS BOTANIC GARDEN

Rock, peat and water gardens, tree, shrub, bulb and herbaceous borders. Glasshouses & wide range of plants.

OPEN

May to September	10 am to 7 pm	7 days a week
October to April	10 am to 4 pm	7 days a week

GLASSHOUSES

May to September	10 am to 4 pm	7 days a week
October to April	10 am to 4 pm	Monday to Friday

ENTRY CHARGES
£1.50   Senior Citizens £1 Children 5–16 50p

The Churches of Scotland

The illustrated Handbook of Scotland's Churches Scheme gives details of Cathedrals, Abbeys and Churches of all denominations open to visitors in 1997.

Visit some of the most exquisite examples of our rich ecclesiastical heritage, enjoy their peace and solace, and help towards their work and mission.

Obtainable from Tourist Information Centres, price £1.50, or by post for £2.50 from: The Director, Scotland's Churches Scheme, Gladstone Court, Canongate, Edinburgh EH8 8BN   Telephone / Fax: 0131 558 8411.

The KILDRUMMY CASTLE GARDENS

in their unique setting were planted about 1904, within the curtain of silver abies and the drapery of larch and tsuga.

The Alpine Garden in the ancient quarry faces south, the Water Garden flows   below.

Plants for sale.

Admission: Adults £2   Children free.
Tea, Coffee, etc.
Car Park: FREE inside hotel entrance
Coach Park: 2nd entrance.

OPEN DAILY—10 a.m. - 5 p.m. APRIL - OCTOBER

Video Room

Play Area

Woodland Walk

Wheelchair Facilities

ALFORD STRATHDON ROAD, ABERDEENSHIRE (A97 off A944)
Coaches or groups – Write or Telephone 019755 71277 and 71203

Loch Melfort Hotel

The finest location on the West Coast of Scotland—Right beside Arduaine Gardens

For relaxing holidays, short breaks and the perfect base for visiting over 20 beautiful gardens large and small.
Stunning views from our lounges and fully ensuite bedrooms.
Enjoy superb cuisine in our dining room or more informal lunches and suppers in our Chartroom Bar – light meals served all day. Parties welcome by appointment.

Spring and Autumn Breaks plus Christmas and New Year Holidays.

AA Inspectors' Hotel of the Year Scotland.

For brochure and tariff contact Loch Melfort Hotel, Arduaine, by Oban, Argyll PA34 4XG
Tel: 01852 200233   Fax: 01852 200214.

Australia's Open Garden Scheme

Going to Australia?

Visit more than 700 of Australia's most beautiful private gardens spread right across the continent. *Australia's Open Garden Scheme Guidebook,* published each August, contains descriptions, dates and directions as well as photographs of a large number of the gardens featured. For further information about the Scheme or to order the Guidebook, please contact our office;

National Executive Officer: Neil Robertson, Westport, New Gisborne, Victoria 3438, Australia Tel: +61 (3) 5428 4557   Fax: +61 (3) 5428 4558

Australia's Open Garden Scheme Limited ACN 057 467 553

INDEX TO GARDENS

INDEX TO ADVERTISERS